The history of Emily Willis, a natural daughter. In two volumes. ... The third edition. Volume 1 of 2

The history of Emily Willis, a natural daughter. In two volumes. ... The third edition. Volume 1 of 2
Multiple Contributors, See Notes
ESTCID: T094635
Reproduction from British Library

London : printed for F. Noble, at his Circulating Library; and J. Noble, at his Circulating Library, 1768.
2v. ; 12°

Eighteenth Century
Collections Online
Print Editions

Gale ECCO Print Editions

Relive history with *Eighteenth Century Collections Online*, now available in print for the independent historian and collector. This series includes the most significant English-language and foreign-language works printed in Great Britain during the eighteenth century, and is organized in seven different subject areas including literature and language; medicine, science, and technology; and religion and philosophy. The collection also includes thousands of important works from the Americas.

The eighteenth century has been called "The Age of Enlightenment." It was a period of rapid advance in print culture and publishing, in world exploration, and in the rapid growth of science and technology – all of which had a profound impact on the political and cultural landscape. At the end of the century the American Revolution, French Revolution and Industrial Revolution, perhaps three of the most significant events in modern history, set in motion developments that eventually dominated world political, economic, and social life.

In a groundbreaking effort, Gale initiated a revolution of its own: digitization of epic proportions to preserve these invaluable works in the largest online archive of its kind. Contributions from major world libraries constitute over 175,000 original printed works. Scanned images of the actual pages, rather than transcriptions, recreate the works *as they first appeared.*

Now for the first time, these high-quality digital scans of original works are available via print-on-demand, making them readily accessible to libraries, students, independent scholars, and readers of all ages.

For our initial release we have created seven robust collections to form one the world's most comprehensive catalogs of 18th century works.

Initial Gale ECCO Print Editions collections include:

History and Geography
Rich in titles on English life and social history, this collection spans the world as it was known to eighteenth-century historians and explorers. Titles include a wealth of travel accounts and diaries, histories of nations from throughout the world, and maps and charts of a world that was still being discovered. Students of the War of American Independence will find fascinating accounts from the British side of conflict.

Social Science
Delve into what it was like to live during the eighteenth century by reading the first-hand accounts of everyday people, including city dwellers and farmers, businessmen and bankers, artisans and merchants, artists and their patrons, politicians and their constituents. Original texts make the American, French, and Industrial revolutions vividly contemporary.

Medicine, Science and Technology
Medical theory and practice of the 1700s developed rapidly, as is evidenced by the extensive collection, which includes descriptions of diseases, their conditions, and treatments. Books on science and technology, agriculture, military technology, natural philosophy, even cookbooks, are all contained here.

Literature and Language
Western literary study flows out of eighteenth-century works by Alexander Pope, Daniel Defoe, Henry Fielding, Frances Burney, Denis Diderot, Johann Gottfried Herder, Johann Wolfgang von Goethe, and others. Experience the birth of the modern novel, or compare the development of language using dictionaries and grammar discourses.

Religion and Philosophy
The Age of Enlightenment profoundly enriched religious and philosophical understanding and continues to influence present-day thinking. Works collected here include masterpieces by David Hume, Immanuel Kant, and Jean-Jacques Rousseau, as well as religious sermons and moral debates on the issues of the day, such as the slave trade. The Age of Reason saw conflict between Protestantism and Catholicism transformed into one between faith and logic -- a debate that continues in the twenty-first century.

Law and Reference
This collection reveals the history of English common law and Empire law in a vastly changing world of British expansion. Dominating the legal field is the *Commentaries of the Law of England* by Sir William Blackstone, which first appeared in 1765. Reference works such as almanacs and catalogues continue to educate us by revealing the day-to-day workings of society.

Fine Arts
The eighteenth-century fascination with Greek and Roman antiquity followed the systematic excavation of the ruins at Pompeii and Herculaneum in southern Italy; and after 1750 a neoclassical style dominated all artistic fields. The titles here trace developments in mostly English-language works on painting, sculpture, architecture, music, theater, and other disciplines. Instructional works on musical instruments, catalogs of art objects, comic operas, and more are also included.

The BiblioLife Network

This project was made possible in part by the BiblioLife Network (BLN), a project aimed at addressing some of the huge challenges facing book preservationists around the world. The BLN includes libraries, library networks, archives, subject matter experts, online communities and library service providers. We believe every book ever published should be available as a high-quality print reproduction; printed on-demand anywhere in the world. This insures the ongoing accessibility of the content and helps generate sustainable revenue for the libraries and organizations that work to preserve these important materials.

The following book is in the "public domain" and represents an authentic reproduction of the text as printed by the original publisher. While we have attempted to accurately maintain the integrity of the original work, there are sometimes problems with the original work or the micro-film from which the books were digitized. This can result in minor errors in reproduction. Possible imperfections include missing and blurred pages, poor pictures, markings and other reproduction issues beyond our control. Because this work is culturally important, we have made it available as part of our commitment to protecting, preserving, and promoting the world's literature.

GUIDE TO FOLD-OUTS MAPS and OVERSIZED IMAGES

The book you are reading was digitized from microfilm captured over the past thirty to forty years. Years after the creation of the original microfilm, the book was converted to digital files and made available in an online database.

In an online database, page images do not need to conform to the size restrictions found in a printed book. When converting these images back into a printed bound book, the page sizes are standardized in ways that maintain the detail of the original. For large images, such as fold-out maps, the original page image is split into two or more pages

Guidelines used to determine how to split the page image follows:

- Some images are split vertically; large images require vertical and horizontal splits.
- For horizontal splits, the content is split left to right.
- For vertical splits, the content is split from top to bottom.
- For both vertical and horizontal splits, the image is processed from top left to bottom right.

12654. cc. 4 f

THE
HISTORY
OF
EMILY WILLIS,
A
NATURAL DAUGHTER.

In TWO VOLUMES.

VOL I.

THE THIRD EDITION.

LONDON

Printed for F NOBLE, at his Circulating
Library, near *Middle-Row Holborn*,
AND
J. NOBLE, at his Circulating Library, in St.
Martin's-Court, near *Leicester-Square*.
MDCCLXVIII.

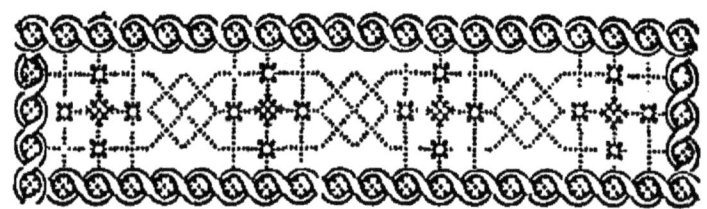

EMILY WILLIS:

OR, THE

HISTORY

OF A

NATURAL DAUGHTER.

BOOK I.

ON a sultry *Saturday*, in the Month of *July*, 1753, about five o'Clock in the Afternoon, the *Turnham-Green Machine* set off from the *White Horse Cellar* in *Piccadilly*, laden with the following Passengers; *viz.* Mr. and Mrs. *Hippocrene*, and their three Daughters, (the eldest not more than Nine Years of Age) Miss *Emily*

Willis, Mrs. *Easy*, and her Maid, and Mr. *Smatter*.

Mr. *Hippocrene* was a Bookseller, and met with Encouragement enough in Business to have kept his Family very tolerably, but an unlucky Fondness for the Character of an Author, and an immoderate Desire to distinguish himself as a Dramatic Poet, seized him early in life, and prevented him from giving that Sort of Attention to his Shop, without which no Trader can ever expect to succeed. His Person, Dress, and Behaviour were equally grotesque. He was very tall and thin, dark-complexioned, hollow-eyed, and beetle-brow'd; his Nose was sharp, his Chin picked, and his Mouth wide, his Coat, Waistcoat and Breeches had once been of a light Cloth Colour, but were so much tinged with Dirt, Dust, and Snuff, that the original Hue was almost obliterated. His Head was adorned with a long yellowish Tye-Wig, out of Curl and unpowdered, which hung gracefully enough upon his Shoulders, when he was not agitated by the *Poetic Frenzy*; but whenever that seized him, or when any Body happened to mention the

the Word *Drama*, or any thing relating to Theatrical Affairs, he always applied the Fore-finger and Thumb of his left Hand to the Foretop of his Periwig, with such Vehemence, that his Nose was in a few Minutes in Danger of being buried in the Cawl of it.

Mrs. *Hippocrene*'s Figure was diametrically opposite to her Husband's, for she was uncommonly short and thick, with a Complexion which plainly shewed, that (though she had a great Passion for Poetry) she was not contented with the Waters of *Helicon*. She was, indeed, a little inconsistent Lump of Affectation, having, from her first Acquaintance with Mr. *Hippocrene*, imbibed high-flown Notions of Things, and acquired a bombastical Manner of expressing her Thoughts upon the most indifferent Subjects, a *Manner* far above the Conception of the Bulk of Mankind. Her Affectation indeed was carried to the most romantic Height, for she had named her three Girls after three of the Muses, and when she was particularly good-humoured, called them her *dear little Irrationals*.

As she always had a prodigious hankering after tufted Groves, verdant Lawns, and purling Streams, her Husband indulged her every Summer with a Country Lodging, and was not less pleased himself to fly from the Smoke and Noise of the Town. *Turnham-Green* was the Spot fixed upon for their Residence at that Time, and thither they were going, for the Benefit of Air and Contemplation.

They lodged in a small Cottage, which was situated very near the High Road, but had a Bit of a Garden behind it, at the Bottom of which, about three Yards from the House, there was a latticed Arbor, covered with Jessamines and Honeysuckles. This Arbor Mrs *Hippocrene* honoured with the Name of *her Fairy Bower*. The Garden joined to a Skittle-Ground on one side, to the Yard of a Dealer in Hogs on the other, and was bounded by an Enclosure for Asses. To this delicious Spot they were going, (as I said before) accompanied by Miss *Emily Willis*, who was under the Guardianship of Mr. *Hippocrene*.

Miss

Miss *Willis* was about eighteen Years of Age, tall and well-shaped, her Complexion was fair, and her Hair brown, but her Features were not quite regular enough to form a complete *Beauty*. There was however such an Expression of Sense and Delicacy in her Face, and so much Modesty and Affability in her Behaviour, that she attracted the Admiration of all who beheld her, and won the Esteem of all who conversed with her.

Mis *Easy* was the Widow of a Gentleman who possest a very genteel and profitable Place under the Government, but was of too extravagant a Turn to think of leaving her in affluent Circumstances. She had indeed barely enough to maintain herself and one Maid, without making a shabby Appearance

This Lady was pretty far advanced in Life, between forty and fifty, and rather disagreeable in her Person (having never had the least Pretensions to Beauty, even in her girlish Days) as she had a Fierceness in her Air, bordering upon the *Masculine*, which she too much affected.

affected. But she had so excellent an Understanding, and knew the World so thoroughly, (having employed her leisure Hours chiefly in acquiring useful and unperishable Accomplishments) that she would at any Time, in half an Hour, *talk away her Person*.

As Mrs. *Easy* was descended from one of the best Families in the Kingdom, and very capable of giving Entertainment in Conversation, her Company was always eagerly solicited, by which Means she had frequent Opportunities of indulging her darling Passion, which was to criticise on the Characters she met with, and the more odd and uncommon they were, the more was she diverted with them; not that she was of an envious, censorious, or malicious Disposition. No Body wished more sincerely to do good, and to communicate Happiness, but her Fondness for Oddities was so excessive, that she would quit the Company of her best Friend, or go without her Dinner, in order to *enjoy a new Character*. It was this Taste for Humour which determined her to take Places in the *Machine*, having been advised by her Physician,

sician, to establish her Recovery from a Fever, by trying the salutary Air of *Turnham-Green.*

Miss *Easy*, as soon as she entered the *sociable Vehicle*, fixed her Eyes on Mr and Mrs. *Hiprocrene*, whom she looked upon as excellent Objects for her, and only took them off now and then, to admire the engaging Simplicity which appeared in the Countenance and Carriage of Miss *Willis.* For though her Amusement rose chiefly from attending to the *Ridiculous*, she was perfectly capable of distinguishing and relishing the *Amiable*, wherever she found it. Her ruling Foible was too great an Adoration of *High Life*, which she had contracted by being related to, and acquainted with, many Families of Fashion. This Foible predominated so much, that she thought the most servile Condition *within their Circle*, preferable to a State of Freedom and Independency *out* of it. This Part of her Character she however knew how to conceal, when it suited her Convenience, having an admirable Knack at accommodating herself to all Ranks and Degrees of People,

A 4   from

from the aukward Rustic to the polish'd Courtier.

The last, and least remarkable Passenger, was Mr *Smatter*, a young Gentleman about five and twenty, possest of a small Place in one of the public Offices. He was one of those *Demi-Smarts* who generally appear in a very scanty Frock, with a narrow Silver Edging, a small Hat, decorated with the same Kind of Trimming, a red and white check'd Linen Waistcoat, and his Hair in a Queue: So much for his outward Form; how to describe the rest of him, I am somewhat at a Loss: He was, in short, half Beau, half Buck, and half Wit; and, to speak properly, had no Character at all. He aimed, notwithstanding, at great things, and was a mighty Frequenter of the Playhouses, especially on those Nights when the Manager, apprehending that the House will not be crouded, (either from the Thinness of the Town, the unexpected Illness of a principal Performer, or some other weighty Reason) distributes *Orders* with a liberal Hand, that he may keep up the Spirits of his Actors and Actresses, and have the Satisfaction

faction of reading, in the following Day's Papers, a Paragraph to this Purpose: Last Night was performed, at *Covent-Garden*, or *Drury-Lane*, such and such a Tragedy, or Comedy, with great Applause, to a very numerous and splendid Audience. As *Smatter* had contracted an Intimacy with some of the Under-Actors, Side-Dancers, &c. &c. &c. he was often complimented with an *Order*, which gave him an Opportunity of shining in the Side-Box now and then; a Place he never would have appeared in at his own Expence. He was, that Afternoon, taking a Walk to *Knightsbridge*, where he kept a Girl snug and cheap, but the accidental Sight of Miss *Willis*, as the Machine stood at the *Cellar*, made him desirous of a little Ride, that he might know if she was really as handsome and agreeable, on a nearer View, as she seemed to be at a Distance.

They had proceeded as far as the Wall of the *Green-Park*, before he thought proper to open his Lips; his Attention had been wholly engrossed, not by the Beauty of the Lady, but by the droll Figure of the Bard, with whom

whom he expected to have *some choice Scenes*. He therefore, after heartily cursing the Dust, addressed himself to the Company in the following Manner:—I have a mortal Aversion to this stupid Time of the Year, for the Town is so empty, that there's nothing stirring; and a Man of Taste may, I vow, as well be annihilated during the Summer Months, when all People of true Genius are dispersed, and no Body left in Town, not a single Person fit to converse with—You say true, Sir, replied the Bard, it is a very desolate Season indeed, but it will soon be over. and when once the Theatres open, we shall be all alive again.—Lard, cried Mrs. *Hippocrene*, I can't conceive how any Creature can complain, with any Propriety, of such a delectable Division of the Year, except indeed they are obliged to spend it in Town, where, to be sure, every Thing is then shocking to the last Degree, but in a rural Retirement, what can be more enchanting than the glowing Warmth of the Meridian Sun, and the fanning Breezes of an Evening Zephyr?

I am

I am quite of your Opinion, Madam, said Mrs. *Easy*, (who rejoiced to hear her open so finely, and wished for nothing more than to draw her out) there is something so very agreeable in our Sensations of every Thing about us in Summer, that I wonder any Person should not prefer it to the Inclemencies of the Winter, in our Climate Unless, continued she, with an Eye to *Hippocrene*, they are Admirers of Theatrical Entertainments, which may certainly be deemed both rational and agreeable.—Ay, cried the Bard, they might be made both rational and agreeable, but at present we have no Body that can write for the Stage, except one or two, and they have met with so little Encouragement, that—

No Body that can write for the Stage, Sir, replied *Smatter*, briskly, why what do you think of *Johnson* and *Whitehead*? for I suppose you mean Tragic Writers. —Undoubtedly, Sir, said *Hippocrene*, undoubtedly, Sir, *Comedy* is nothing at all, it requires no Genius, any Body may write a *Comedy*. As to the Gentlemen you mentioned, why I own they are tolerable Dabblers enough in Tragedy. I don't love to depreciate any Man, not I. But if you could see the Tragedies *I* have wrote, Sir, I believe, without Vanity, that you would be of another Opinion —Perhaps I might be of another Opinion, Sir, said *Smatter*, but pray let me ask the favour of your Name?—My Name, Sir, is *Hippocrene*, at your Service.—*Hippocrene!* replied *Smatter*, *Hippocrene!* I don't remember ever to have heard of it before.—May be not, Sir, answered the Bard, in a Pet, may be not, but I am known, Sir, I can assure you.—Yes, thank Heaven, said Mrs *Hippocrene*, we have not been all our Lives buried in Obscurity. Mr. *Hippocrene* and I have distinguished ourselves, nobly distinguished ourselves.

Smatter was ready to burst with Laughter at the Fuss he had put the Lady in, and at the Commotion of her Spouse, which was easily to be perceived in the latter, by the violent Application of his Left-Hand to his Fore-top, but tried to compose himself as well as he could. Hem! Pray Sir, said he to the Bard, after thrusting his Tongue into a Corner a Corner of his Cheek, and rolling his Eyes at Miss *Willis*, (Tricks which he had caught by endeavouring to *take off* a celebrated Comedian) were these same Tragedies of yours ever acted?— Acted, Sir? said *Hippocrene*; no, Sir, I told you People of Genius met with little Encouragement, but I have almost finished a *Piece*, which I design to bring upon the Stage next Winter, that will, I believe, render the Name of *Hippocrene* as well known as the immortal *Shakespear*'s—Pray, Sir, said *Smatter*, which House is to be honoured with your new Production?—Lord, Sir, cried *Hippocrene*, what a Question is that!—*Drury-Lane*, to be sure, there are no Actors at t'other House, no Actors at all. You must know, Sir, I have wrote a Part on Purpose for Mr. *Garrick*; I wish I had it about me (continued he, feeling in his Pockets for it) *Hannah*, said he to his Wife, I gave it to you just before I came out, to put in your Box; where is the Key? —Lard, Mr. *Hippocrene*, cried she, you certainly are guilty of an exceeding gross Mistake. I have not one individual Thing in my Box, but the first Book of my own Pastorals, which you

may

may shew the Gentleman if you please —'Sdeath and Hell, replied he, then I have left it at Home, and must return for it directly. Here, Coachman, set me down this Minute.—Pshaw, prithee Mr *Hippocrene*, said his lovely Helpmate, don't think of getting out here, you will indubitably too much inflame yourself by walking so far. As Tomorrow, you know, is *Sunday*, you may take a Trip, and fetch it before Breakfast.—That wont do, cried he, staring like a Mad-man, that wont do; for I always chuse to exercise my Pen in the cool of the Morning. 'Sdeath, what a vexatious Accident!

Pray, Sir, (said *Smatter*,) who rejoiced secretly that his Piece was not to be found, and wanted to hinder him from fetching it) what may the Title of your Play be?—The Title, Sir, answered he, is in my humble Opinion, a very magnificent one, for it is *The Assembly of the Gods*.—Umph, said *Smatter*, winking at Miss *Willis*, that is quite new, I must confess, then I suppose your Characters——My Characters, interrupted the Bard, are those Cœlestial Personages, *Jupiter, Apollo, Mars, Neptune, Vulcan*,
and

and *Mercury*, Males, *Juno, Venus, Pallas*, and *Diana*, Females. Now, Sir, I will give my Reasons for chusing this Subject. In the first Place, because it was out of the common Track of Writing. The Town has long been tired of the Stories of Kings and Princes; besides, if a private History was wrought into a Play, though ever so affecting, how apt is every Body to say, Why to be sure it is natural, but they are so very low, that there is no enduring it. The Dignity of the Stage, Sir, must be kept up, and how can that be done more effectually than by introducing such illustrious Characters? You shall hear now in what a majestic Manner I bring on the tremendous Thunderer in the first Scene. I believe I can recollect two or three of his sublime Speeches.

Hold, hold, Sir, interrupted *Scatter*, before you begin to repeat, I should be glad to know how you have cast the Parts. I suppose this tremendous Gentleman is to be represented by Mr. *Garrick*.—No, Sir, no, said *Hippocrene*, I pay him a much greater Compliment, I think, by giving him *Apollo*, the God of of Wit and Poesy. O that I had but my Piece about me! You can't imagine, Sir, how I have touch'd up *Apollo*'s Part, in order to shew his Representative to Advantage. No, no, *Jove* is too blustering a Character. There is an Elegance, a Delicacy in all Mr. *Garrick*'s Performances, accompanied with such Spirit and Propriety, that render him the Delight of our Stage. I have therefore prick'd him down for *Apollo*, who is every way a fine Gentleman.—Why, said *Smatter*, my Friend *Garrick* is certainly a pretty Player, a very pretty Player.—What do you mean by a *very pretty Player?* cried Mrs *Easy:* (whose Indignation rose at the affected Importance of this Coxcomb, and at his calling a Man, whom he had not Courage to speak to, with so much Familiarity, his Friend,) I have seen, Sir, Mr *Booth*, Mr *Wilks*, and Mr. *Cibber*, and have conversed with those who saw *Mountfort* and *Betterton*. These were all eminent Actors, but I am fully persuaded that there never was so universal a Genius as Mr. *Garrick*. Was either of these Gentlemen capable of shining in a *Lear* and a *Bays*, a *Hamlet* and a *Drugger*, a *Macbeth* and a *Fribble?*

Characters

Characters widely different from each other, and yet they are all supported with the greatest Spirit, and the exactest Propriety, by that Man whom you slightly call *a very pretty Player*.

Smatter had fixed his Eyes full upon her during her Encomiums on his *Friend Garrick*, but at the Conclusion of it, twisted his Lips into a long Wh---ew, and, putting his Head out at the Window, said to the Driver, You thick-skull'd Rascal, why didn't you stop where I bid you? You have carried me, Sirrah, a Mile out of my Way. Here, set me down this Moment. Upon this rough Salutation, the Driver got down and opened the Door. *Smatter* then whipp'd out like a Harlequin, noddled his Head, bowed carelesly at the Company, leered particularly at Miss *Willis*, and then shuffled away to his *Dulcinea*.

Hippocrene, who had only been detained by *Smatter*'s Enquiries relating to his *Performance*, immediately followed him, in Spite of all his Wife's Intreaties to postpone his Walk till the next Morning. He declared that the finest Thought in the Universe just popped into

into his Head, and that if he did not hurry, and clap it down in Black and White, it might be irrecoverably loft, and, without waiting for a Reply, disappeared in a Moment.

As soon as he was gone, Mrs. *Eafy*, who had waited very impatiently to hear Mifs *Willis*'s Voice, but in vain, made an Effort to draw *her* out too, by afking her where fhe was to be fet down. *Emily* anfwered, I am at prefent, Madam, with Mrs. *Hippocrene*.— Aye, Madam, faid the Poetefs, Mifs *Willis* is under my Confort's Protection, he is her Guardian.—What has fhe neither Father nor Mother? replied Mrs. *Eafy*. —No, Madam, Mifs never knew her paternal or maternal Relations, nor indeed does any Body elfe know who they were.

Mrs. *Eafy*'s Curiofity was very much heightened by this Speech, but as fhe perceived that *Emily*'s Face was covered with Blufhes, and that her Eyes were full of Tears, fhe refolved to defer the Gratification of it till a more proper Opportunity: And, in order to give the amiable Girl Time to recover herfelf, changed

changed the Conversation, by asking Mis *Hippocrene* if she intended to spend the Remainder of the Summer in the Country. O certainly, cried she, I am quite an Inamorata with rural Solitude, I fly to sequestered Places for the Benefit of Reflection. One has no Time, no Power to reflect in Town, where there is such a Contrariety of ridiculous Objects, and such a Tumult of dissonant Sounds.—You are in the right, Madam, replied Mis *Easy*, (smiling at her Phraseology) but I suppose when Mr *Hippocrene*'s Tragedy is in Rehearsal, he will be obliged to attend the *House*, and you will also, without doubt, be anxious for the Success of it.—As to the *Success* of it, Madam, said Mrs. *Hippocrene*, screwing up her Mouth, and fidgeting in her Seat, I believe no Body has the least Suspicion; not but that he might have done better, if he had taken my Advice, but he is so opinionated, that he never will be open to Conviction. I can't for my Soul persuade him to erase a Line, or else his *Juno* would have been *marked* beyond any thing you ever met with. Would you credit it, Madam? I penn'd the whole Part of *Juno* myself, and I vow there

was

was an infinite deal of Majesty in it, yet he woudn't insert it——not he.

'Tis a great Pity indeed, said Mis *Easy*, that he will not follow your Advice; were I in his Place, I should think myself very happy in being wedded to a Woman capable of assisting me.—O Madam, replied she, your Observation is a very accurate one, I can truly say, that he never would have gained the Summit of *Parnassus* without my Assistance, I have done a thousand Things to raise his Family, which he would never have thought of.

As for our Daughters, whom I have called after the Muses——How, Madam, said Mrs. *Easy*, have you nine Children?—No, Madam, answered Mis. *Hippocrene*, the Fates have yet allotted me but these three, (pointing at them) but I hope that Mr *Hippocrene* and I, shall, by our conjunctive Endeavours, equal the Number of the *Heliconian* Virgins.

Though Mrs. *Easy* was very expert at keeping her Countenance, she could not, at the Close of this Speech, stifle a vioa violent Fit of Laughing, which might have given great Offence, had not the sudden Appearance of a Gentleman at the Window of the *Machine*, with a Sword in his Hand, engrossed the whole Attention of the Speaker of it. This Gentleman was Mr *Hopwou'd*, a Dancing-Master, Mrs *Hippocrene*'s Brother, who had been invited to stay with her at her *Villa*, from *Saturday* to *Monday*, for Reasons which will hereafter be disclosed.

Mr *Hopwou'd* was almost as short and as thick as his Sister, but appeared more conspicuously aukward, because he was preposterously habited. He was drest in a light-brown, Metal-button'd *Manchester*-Velvet Coat, a dirty white Waistcoat stitch'd with Yellow, which just touch'd the Waistband of a Pair of Scarlet-Shagg Breeches, over which were rolled the Superfluities of a Pair of white Worsted Stockings, an old Weather-beaten Queue-Wig, and a tarnish'd Gold-lac'd Hat, standing bolt upright, covered his Head, and exposed to View, a jolly, round, unthinking Face, pitted and seamed frightfully by the Small-Pox, and rendered more flame-

flame-colour'd than usual, by the Acceleration of his Velocity to overtake the Vehicle. This uncouth Figure, after saluting Mrs *Hippocrene* and the Company, placed himself, with all the Familiarity in the World, by the Side of *Emily*, to whom he complained heavily of the violent Sweat he was in, declaring that he had suffered more Fatigue in the last Hour, than in a whole Afternoon's Teaching.

Mrs. *Easy*, who had, at first Sight, as cordial a Contempt for *Hopwou'd*, as she before had for *Smatter*, soon found that Miss *Willis*, in whose Favour she began to be prejudiced, was far from being pleased with his Company. She therefore very obligingly seated herself on the other Side of the young Lady, and entered into Chat with her about common Things, not only to hear if she answered her Expectation, but to relieve her Modesty, which apparently suffered not a little, from the near Approaches of her impertinent Neighbour. Soon did she find that *Emily* was deserving of her highest Esteem, and invited her to her Lodgings the next Day. *Emily* only replied with a Bow, and a
Look

Look at Mrs *Hippocrene*, as if she waited for *her* Consent. Miss *Easy* observing her Suspence, immediately desired that Lady to give Miss *Willis* Leave to favour her with her Company. To-morrow, Madam, said Mrs. *Hippocrene*, Miss *Emily* knows she is engaged, but she shall wait on you on *Monday*. This Speech gave *Emily* a Satisfaction which she could not conceal. She tried by several little engaging Ways to render herself more and more agreeable to Mrs. *Easy*, and to let her see how much she thought herself obliged to her, for taking such Notice of her.

While Mrs. *Easy* and *Emily* were engaged in Conversation, Mrs. *Hippocrene* talk'd away a great deal to her Brother, about her Husband's Play, and twenty other Things of equal Importance, without any Interruption; for as his Excellence, if he had any, lay diametrically opposite to his Head, he was very indifferently qualified for shining in Conversation. He amused himself, therefore, with whistling a Minuet, squeezing *Emily*'s Hand tenderly, and crying out every now and then, Ha, my sweet little Rogue, how dost do? But

But his Fondnesses were repeated so often, that *Emily* began to lose all Patience, and shewed her Dislike to them by withdrawing her Hand, turning hastily from him, and making no Answer. These Signals of Aversion rouzed Mrs. *Hippocrene*'s Resentment, who could not bear to see her Brother slighted. Indeed, *Miss*, (said she to her) you give yourself very lofty Airs, which by no Means accord with your Situation, but I shall embrace the first Opportunity to apprize your Guardian of your Proceedings; and if he wont take proper Notice of you, I'll teach you myself, by *Juno, the venerable Ox-ey'd Juno*, another System of Behaviour. Poor *Emily* blush'd at this Reprimand, but made no Reply; it entirely deprived her of that Chearfulness she had just begun to assume; nor could Mrs. *Easy*, who pitied her Situation, and continued to prattle to her, remove the Chagrin it had occasioned.

Soon after this Incident, they arrived at the End of their Journey When the *Machine* stopt at the Poet's Habitation, the gallant Mr. *Hopwou'd* offered his Hand to Miss *Willis*, who curtsied very respectfully to Mrs. *Easy*, and received

ceived another invitation from her, which she promised to comply with Mis *Hippocrene*, finding that the abovementioned Lady had omitted to invite *her*, either by Design, or through Forgetfulness, would not take Leave without saying, Mr. *Hippocrene*, Madam, will, I am sure, take great Pleasure in reading his *Piece* to you, if you have any Inclination to hear it, and will grace our *Fairy Bower* with your Presence. In answer to this Flourish, Mrs. *Easy* only said, *I am much obliged to you, Madam*, and proceeded to her Lodgings, glad to be at Liberty to laugh at the Variety of original Characters she had left behind.

Mrs. *Easy*, notwithstanding her violent Passion for Humour, interested herself so much in *Emily*'s Affairs, that she could scarce turn her Thoughts to any Thing else. She waited impatiently for *Monday* Afternoon. When the wish'd-for Hour arrived, she welcomed her new Visitor with Smiles and Affability, and after the Tea-table was removed, addressed her in the following Manner.

I am going, Miſs *Willis*, to take great Liberties with you, but I am inclined to believe you will not be diſpleaſed, when you are acquainted with the real Motive of them. I cannot help fancying but that you are leſs happy than you deſerve to be. I ſhould be glad to know, (if you can venture to put ſo much Confidence in me, upon ſo ſhort an Acquaintance) how you came to be placed among the *Hippocrenes*—Perhaps I may be of Service to you *Emily*'s Cheeks glowed at the Cloſe of this Speech Mrs *Eaſy* perceived her Uneaſineſs with Concern, and thus went on Don't be alarmed, my Dear, I will not be offended with your ſilence. My Curioſity, (though I aſſure you 'tis a friendly one) may perhaps be improper: But I dare ſay you will gratify it when we are more intimate.—You are very obliging, Madam, ſaid *Emily*, (who ſoon recovered from her Confuſion) to ſhew me ſo much Kindneſs I ſhould be very ready to tell you all that I know of myſelf, without the leaſt Heſitation, were I not afraid of making you, thereby, think leſs favourably of me. I can truly ſay I am innocent, though I am ſo unhappy as never to

have

have known my Parents. I can only remember that I was put, very young, to a great Boarding-School, by one Mrs. *Dawson*, who paffed for my Aunt. She was very fond of me, and treated me in the moft affectionate Manner· At the Times of *Breaking-up* I always ftayed with her, during the Holidays, at her Houfe in *Westminster*, and fhe fo bountifully provided for me at School, that I made as genteel an Appearance as any of my Companions did. By her Order I learnt Dancing, *French*, Mufick and Drawing; of the laft, particularly, I became excefsively fond, having ftudied it under the Care and Direction of that able and judicious Mafter, Mr. *Bonneau*, fo juftly efteemed, by all true Judges of Merit, for his excellent Manner of Teaching, and who flattered me I made a great Proficiency in that agreeable Art.

I know not how long, Madam, I might have ftaid at School, had not Mr *Dawson*, whom I called Uncle, died, when I was about fifteen. I was then fent for, and remained at Home a Year, where I lived happily, and had every thing I wanted. All my Care was to please Mrs. *Dawson*, whose affectionate Behaviour to me deserved every Return I could make. One day she was suddenly taken ill. A Physician was sent for, who declared she had all the Symptoms of an Apoplexy, and gave us no Hopes of her Recovery. I was extremely afflicted with this News, and attended her with the Assiduity of a dutiful Child. While I was sitting by her Bed-side one Afternoon, she took hold of my Hand, looked tenderly at me, and thus unbosomed herself. My dear *Emmy*, though you are an humane amiable Girl, and love me, I believe, as well as if I was really your Aunt—Good God, Madam, cried I, astonished, why are you not my Aunt? No, replied she, I am no way related to you. You may easily imagine how much this Speech, which she delivered in the calmest Manner, surprized me. I thought, indeed, that her Disorder had seized her Head, and offered to fetch something for her to take. Stay, Child, said she, I am better than I was, but I may be worse again, and therefore, as you are both old and discreet enough to be trusted with a Secret, listen to me with Attention. But first see if the Door is fast,

that

that no Body may interrupt us. I obeyed, and promised to do every Thing she would have me, if she would tell me who my Parents were, and why I had been so long deprived of the Satisfaction of knowing them. I cannot, said she, tell you who your Parents were, without being guilty of Perjury, but I will inform you in what Manner you came into the World, and how little you are to expect from it. I trembled at this alarming Introduction, but was however desirous of hearing every Thing she thought proper to tell me, and begged her earnestly to proceed.

Your Mother, said she, was Daughter to a Gentleman of Family and Fortune in the North of *England*, and an Heiress. Her Education was suitable to the Fortune she expected, which, added to the Beauty and Gentility of her Person, gained her numberless Admirers, but her Father, resolving that she should not marry beneath herself, was very cautious about chusing a Husband for her. Whilst he was looking out for a proper Match, a young *Scots* Officer of good Extraction, who had nothing to subsist on but his Pay, became acquainted

ed in the Family, and engaged your Mother's Affections (as he had many agreeable Accomplishments to recommend him to a Woman's Esteem) nor was he long insensible to her Youth and Beauty. They made use of every Opportunity in their Power to enjoy each other's Company, and grew at last so careless about their Meetings, that the old Gentleman discovered them, and fell into a violent Passion thereupon, forbidding the Captain his House, and threatening your Mother, that he would disinherit her if she ever saw him again. Your Mother was frighted at this Menace, which she firmly believed he would put in Execution, and therefore wrote an Account of it to her Lover, telling him at the same Time, that he must not think either to see her, or even to write to her again. He sent her in Return a long Letter, in which he begged she would consent to go off with him, and be privately married, assuring her he had no Doubt of her Father's being reconciled, when his Passion subsided, and giving her a Hint about making a fair Discovery of her Situation to him, in order to procure his Consent. But she rejected all his Proposals, and plainly
told

told him that there were no Hopes of her Father's being ever brought to hear of them with Patience, and persisted in her first Resolution to break off all Acquaintance with him; refusing to receive the Letters and Messages he contrived to send her while he stayed in the Country, which was about a Month, he was then ordered to go with the Regiment to *Minorca*. As soon as he left *England*, she contrived that her Father should immediately hear of it, and then desired Leave to come to *London*. He readily complied with her Request, when he knew the Captain was embarked, and she concealed her growing Disorder so well, that he had no Suspicions, but redoubled his Kindness to her, as a Recompence for her quitting the Captain at his Desire.

When your Mother arrived in Town, she came directly to me, and inform'd me of her Condition. I then concerted Measures for her Lying-in privately, which succeeded very well. When every Thing was prepared, and the expected Time drew near, she pretended to be very ill with a violent Cold and Tooth-ach, and kept her Bed. By the Assistance of a faithful Maid-Servant, a Midwife was introduced in the Night when all the Family were asleep, and she was soon delivered safely of you. She instantly committed you to my Care, and constantly supplied me with Money sufficient for your Subsistence, and for your Education, which she desired might be equal to your Birth. For the Space of two Years she saw you frequently at my House unsuspected, as you past for the Daughter of one of my Sisters, who died when you were born: But her Father then pitch'd upon a Man of Fashion, with a Fortune equal to that which he intended to leave to her. She made a faint Refusal at first, but consented to be married, when she found that he was determined to disinherit her, if she complied not with his Will. Before her Wedding-Day, she took her Farewel of you, and, putting a Purse of Guineas in my Hand, earnestly begged that I would never forsake you, and made me take a solemn Oath, to keep her Secret for ever, even from yourself, till you were old enough to be trusted with it, and even *then*, on no Account whatever, to discover who were the real Authors of your Birth.

Birth. She has never seen you, nor enquired after you since her Marriage, but I should have thought myself guilty of the highest Ingratitude, if I had in any Shape neglected you. I have taken all possible Care of your Education, faithfully kept her Secret, and loved you as my own Child, but I am afraid I shall not long be able to look after you. If Mr *Dawson* had lived, we might have saved something more from the Income of his *Place* for you. However, that's a vain Wish! I shall soon follow him I believe, but a Thousand Pounds will be yours when you are of Age. That's all I can spare from my own Relations, 'till then you may board with Mr *Hippocrene*, who, you know, is my first Cousin, and who will, I doubt not, be kind to you, out of Respect to my Memory, for *he* is also ignorant of your Parents, and must remain so. But why, said I, sighing, why may not *I* be trusted with a Secret which concerns me so much? I shall reveal it to no Body, the Knowledge of it cannot surely be prejudicial to me. There are particular Reasons for my Silence, replied she, therefore be content with what you have already

heard

heard, and enquire no farther. As she delivered this Speech with unusual Harshness, I made no Answer but with my Tears, which I could not check. I was indeed shocked at feeling myself in so distressful a Situation. My Heart, melted with Gratitude towards Mrs. *Dawson*, my amiable Protectress, who I feared would soon leave me to the wide World, in which I should have no Friend, no Relation to comfort me.— *Emily* stopt here—her Tears would not let her proceed. Mrs. *Easy*, who was pleased with the artless Manner in which she told her Story, and pitied her extremely, said and did all she could to raise her drooping Spirits, and then desired her to go on.

Mrs. *Dawson*'s Answer, Madam, continued *Emily*, harsh as it was, did not however intimidate me. I press'd her, whenever she was able to listen to me, to tell me all I wish'd to know. Perhaps, said I to her one Day, this Mother, who was so kind to me in my Childhood, and provided for my Education, may be pleased to hear that her Tenderness and Generosity have not been quite thrown away: You have often

often bestowed Encomiums on my little Performances, and if I could be introduced privately to her, I might possibly receive her Approbation of my past, and Directions for my future Conduct Sure *Emmy*, replied Mrs. *Dawson*, you are very ignorant, indeed, or else out of your Senses, to think she can bear the Sight of such a Daughter at this Time, without being excessively shocked, as she has Children by her Husband. Why so, Madam, said I, am I not as nearly related to her as they are? And have I not as good a Right to her Affection as they have? Why must I be deprived of the Tenderness which others receive? 'Tis very hard that Innocence should suffer so much. Thus I complained, but to no Purpose. When she was in high Spirits, she only laughed at me, when her Illness lowered them, she was either silent, or else desired me to leave her, and not make her melancholy.

Two or three Months pass'd in this Manner, at the End of which my generous Friend died. She left me in her Will, (wherein I was mentioned as the Daughter of a dear Friend of her's deceas'd)

ceas'd) a Thousand Pounds, and appointed Mr. *Hippocrene* my Guardian, till I was one and twenty. I was extremely grieved at her Death, for I lost a sincere Friend. But my Sorrow was considerably increased, when I reflected that the Knowledge of my Parents perished with her; for neither Mrs *Hippocrene*, nor a Nephew of Mrs *Dawson*'s, who inherited what she left, knew the Name or Story of my Mother. As this Nephew and his Wife soon came to take Possession, I was removed by Mr. and Mrs *Hippocrene* to their House. During the first Fortnight I was too much lost in Affliction to attend to their Manners, but found out, in a short Time, that they were very unsuitable to my Taste. While my dear Friend Mrs. *Dawson* lived, she was always conferring Favours upon them, and they had the Art to conceal a great many of their Ways from her, which they thought she would find Fault with, knowing how apt she was to speak her Mind plainly about every Thing. But before *me* they threw off all Restraint, so that I led an unhappy Life with them. Mr. *Hippocrene* told me he would use me like a Friend, and take no more
than

than thirty Pounds a Year for my Board. I was shock'd at the Extravagance of his Demand, and desired that I might go to learn some Sort of Trade, that I might be able to furnish myself with Apparel, and enjoy a little Pocket-money, (for what a paultry Sum, you know, Madam, is five Pounds, for the Supply of a Woman's Dress, even in the most decent and frugal Manner?) He constantly refused to grant my Request, and whenever I asked him how he thought I must live, said, O there are numberless Ways—you would be very silly to part with any of your Money, for I doubt not but you'll soon get a good Husband. Mrs. *Hippocrene* seconds him, and has introduced a Brother of her's, one *Hopwou'd*, for my Dancing-master, whom she would fain have me receive as a Lover also, but I have shewn my Dislike to him so much, that Mr. *Hippocrene* told me Yesterday, he would not pay me my Fortune, unless I married the man he had chosen for me. From these Causes, Madam, the Melancholy arises, which you have so kindly endeavoured to alleviate, but which can never be removed while I am in the Power of thefe People.—Here Mifs *Willis* paufed.

Mrs. *Eafy*, after thanking her for the Relation of her Story, faid, Indeed, my Dear, I am very forry you are fallen into fuch bad Hands; yet don't defpair of getting you fome Relief. As to your Birth, there is nothing particular in it. You are blamelefs, but I cannot approve of your Situation with the *Hippocrenes* by any Means, nor of your going into Bufinefs if he fhould confent. That Face of yours would fubject you to a thoufand Inconveniencies in fuch an expofed Way of Life. The Dancing-mafter is a Wretch not to be endured, befides, if he was ever fo deferving, an Alliance with the Bard's Family muft be both difagreeable and difadvantageous. I have therefore another Scheme for you. How fhould you like to live with a Woman of Fafhion as a Companion? You have had a genteel Education; your Income is fufficient for Cloaths, and, with the Addition of Prefents, if you behave well, you may make a pretty Figure. I am known to feveral Families, to which fuch an agreeable Girl as you wou'd be very acceptable:

acceptable: If you approve of my Proposal, I'll recommend you; but I wou'd not have you determine in Favour of it without taking Time to consider.

Dear Madam, replied *Emily*, how very good you are to me! There is no Occasion for the least Demur. I can determine, at once, in Favour of so agreeable a Way of Life, and shall always look upon you as my best Friend, for proposing it.—I hope, my Dear, said Mrs *Easy* you will meet with no Disappointments in it. You will thereby have an Opportunity of seeing and conversing with the best Company, which is quite necessary to form a young Mind: You will be treated like a Gentlewoman, and have nothing to do but to be good-humour'd and obliging to the Person you are with. But we should have the Consent of your Guardian, otherwise, he may be very troublesome.— I'll do my utmost to procure it, Madam, said *Emily*, and believe I could easily succeed, were it not for Mrs. *Hippocrene*, who seems resolved to make me accept of her Brother —Well, said Mrs *Easy*, I would advise you to acquaint them both

both with the Scheme I have proposed to you, as soon as you can, in order to see how they relish it; if you find them greatly averse to it, drop some Hints about chusing another Guardian, for I fancy they will have a good Effect. *Emily* returned her new Friend a thousand Thanks, for interesting herself in her Affairs, and took her Leave, with a Promise to follow her Advice to a Tittle.

Emily found neither Mr. nor Mrs. *Hippocrene* at Home, the former being gone to read his Play to a neighbouring Bard, and the latter to sit by and criticize upon it. As they did not return till late in the Evening, nothing passed between them material enough to be inserted in this History. Mr. *Hippocrene* was obliged to go to Town early the next Morning to attend his Shop, but as his Lady was extremely fond of her Pillow, *she* and her young Family did not meet at Breakfast before the Clock had struck *eleven*; and even then, that regular Assemblage of the Tea and Bread and Butter, so common in most Houses, was not to be discerned among these extraordinary Children Mrs. *Hippocrene*

Hippocrene herself was a great Enemy to Tea, which she called a ridiculous Slop in a Morning, and used to say that it was an *inebriating Infusion, capable of engendering nothing but the Spleen.* A Liquor, she would add, utterly unknown to the Antients (for whose Customs she had a profound Veneration.) But as she could not tell what they substituted in the room of it, and had often in vain sighed after Nectar and Ambrosia, she chose a Sip of some Liquid which had, in her Opinion, the nearest Resemblance to the *Lacedæmonian* Black-Broth. She therefore regaled herself with a good Pint of Porter, in which she soaked a Nut-brown Toast, well spiced with Nutmeg, and sweetened with the coarsest Sugar. This delectable Cordial, however, was, she thought, both too potent and too palatable for her delicate Offspring, whom she indulged only with Water-Gruel in its purest State. *Emily*, though not fond of this salutary Repast, was obliged to share it with them, or to wait till Dinner, which seldom proved more inviting. Let the Reader suppose them all assembled to take their Morning Beverage, which was served up on a three

legged

legged Joint-stool. Mrs *Hippocrene* herself sat in a low matted Chair, with a Pewter Pot before her, which contained her favourite Mixtures. She was arrayed in a short, scanty Bed-gown, not to be compared with Snow, Alabaster, or Ivory. Her uncomb'd Locks (just escaped from under a double Clout, which the Heat of the Weather, and the Effluvia's rising from her own Bosom, had compelled her to unpin, tho' some straggling Hairs had before made their Appearance through two large Holes at the Top of it) were as glossy as the Wing of the Raven, and flowed carelessly adown her Shoulders. *Melpomene*, the eldest Daughter, received *her* Allowance in a black-and-yellow round Pan with one Ear; the two younger ones, *Clio* and *Calliope*, scrambled together with their Ocamy Spoons, in a broken white Porringer, not much unlike a certain Utensil which Decency forbids me to mention. *Emily*, by not being related to the Family, had the Privilege of a whole glazed brown Bason. Such was the Variety of Mrs. *Hippocrene*'s Breakfast-Equipage.

While

While they were solacing themselves in this Manner, Mrs *Hippocrene* thus directed her Discourse to *Emily*: I was not at Leisure, last Night, Miss, to ask you about Mrs. *Easy*, to know what she said to you, and when she will honorate our Bower with her Presence — She behaved very obligingly, Madam, said *Emily*, and was so kind as to make an advantageous Proposal to me, which I intend to comply with, if you and Mr. *Hippocrene* will give me Leave.— A Proposal, Child, replied Mrs *Hippocrene*, what do you mean? Don't you know that you are as good as betrothed to my Brother?— No, Madam, said *Emily*, but this was quite of a different Nature, it was to—How! interrupted the Poetess: Have you fallen into vile Hands already? Can a Woman, who has so much the Appearance of a Person not deduc'd from the vulgar Herd, have the Effrontery to propose Indecencies to you?— No, dear Madam, said *Emily*, you mistake my Meaning, it did not relate to Marriage.—— Marriage! replied Mrs *Hippocrene*, in a great Hurry of Spirits: No, no, Miss, I don't suppose it did. But you shall not associate with her again, I'll prevent all future Connection

nection, I warrant. What, shall a Virgin, intrusted to the Care of Mr. *Hippocrene* and myself, be grossly contaminated? Chaste *Diana*, forbid!

Indeed, Madam, said *Emily*, you don't understand me —Not understand you, Child? replied Mrs *Hippocrene*, craning up her Head with a contemptuous Laugh, I believe there is no Deficiency in my Intellectuals, thank Heaven! Yes, yes, my Understanding is extremely perfect: It would be something prodigious, if such an illiterate young Thing as You, could pose *me*—Not understand you indeed!—Pray Miss, learn to treat your Superiors with more Respect.— I am very sorry if I have expressed myself improperly, Madam, said *Emily*; but if you are inclined to hear me, I will inform you.—You inform *me*, Girl? I would have you to know, that it is not in your Power to inform *me* —— I am possest of an infinite Deal of Knowledge, and therefore cannot be informed by *you*, who, as I said before, are very ignorant and illiterate. Not but that, I believe, you might in Process of Time, by the great Fatigue of your Preceptors, and your own intense
Appli-

Application, be brought juſt to comprehend the Superficies of Things. But you have hitherto ſhewn no Propenſity to be inſtructed Tho' when you become Mrs. *Hopwou'd,* I hope you will aſſume a more Matron-like Deportment, and carry yourſelf with Dignity.—But, Madam, cried *Emily,* who began to be tired of her running on ſo wildly, Mrs. *Eaſy* knows a Lady of Faſhion, who will receive me as her Companion, and I think I ought not to refuſe ſo advantageous an Offer. As to being married, I am too young to——And pray what is your Objection to be married in the *Aurora* of Life? Is not Youth the proper Seaſon for marrying? ſaid Mrs. *Hippocrene.* Wou'd you ſtay till you are incapable of Propagation? But that is not the Reaſon, Miſs; you don't think my Brother good enough, I ſuppoſe, you have nouriſhed a Flame for another Perſon: But you can't diſpoſe of your Hand without my Huſband's Conſent, except you have a Mind to relinquiſh your Fortune, I aſſure you.—Upon my Word, Madam, ſaid *Emily,* I have encouraged no Body: I am not acquainted with any Man but Mr. *Hippocrene* and Mr. *Hopwou'd.* I have no Inclination

for

for a married Life, but suppose I had, how must I live with Mr *Hopwou'd*, who has not above three Scholars? for you know the Interest of my Money is very inconsiderable, and not sufficient to maintain a Family.

Well, well, replied Mrs. *Hippocrene*, we must make Allowances for the Season, every Body of Taste and Fashion is revelling now in rural Shades, but at the Return of Winter he will get a whole School. And when Mr. *Hippocrene*'s Play comes upon the Stage, we shall prevail on Mr. *Garrick* to retain him as a Side-Dancer: Then *Emmy*, you and he may lodge and board with us, as you will be Friends and Relations: We shall favour you greatly, and be contented with something less than a Hundred a Year.——O, dear Madam, said *Emily*, your Scheme will never do: Mrs. *Easy*'s is far more eligible; for I shall have nothing to pay for my Board in the Family she recommends me to, and in which, I hope, by a little Œconomy, to appear genteel, and to lay up a Trifle every Year.—Ay, to be sure, answered Mrs. *Hippocrene*, you'll be an excellent Œconomist! Why, I question whether

whether you comprehend the true Meaning, the Etymology of the Word · It is derived either from the *Latin* or the *Greek*, I can't, myself, just now, determine which—So, Madam, interrupted *Emily*, I must beg the Favour of you to procure my Guardian's Consent.—Indeed, but I shall not be guilty of so palpable an Indiscretion, replied she; wou'd a young Virgin, so liberally educated as you have been, desert her Guardian, throw herself into the Power of a Stranger, and submit to the ignominious Appellation of a Waiting-Maid, a Kind of upper Servant? Indeed, Miss *Willis*, you are unaccountably imprudent, but I don't impute your Imprudence to any mental Depravity, but to Want of Knowledge; and, let me tell you, Ignorance is a most terrifying Calamity.

I have no Design to throw myself out of my Guardian's Power, Madam, said *Emily*, he will still have the Disposal of me and my little Fortune till I am of Age; but I think he can frame no reasonable Objection to my being agreeably settled —Ay, said Mrs *Hippocrene*, you might have been agreeably settled

settled indeed with my Brother, but you are quite blind to your own Interest; though I am sure Mr. *Hippocrene* will never agree to this extravagant Project of yours —Then you know, Madam, said *Emily*, I can chuse another Guardian.

O can you so, Madam? But I believe you are mistaken. By all the Gods and Goddesses you would make a pretty Fool of yourself, but I shall take Care to inform Mr. *Hippocrene* of your Intentions. Another Guardian, indeed! If such a Thing is practicable, I am sure there is a virulent Deficiency in our Laws. It was not so among the *Greeks* and *Romans*: But in such a piddling Place as *England*, I can't say what may be done. The divine *Astrea*'s judicial Ballance preponderates not over our Heads, as it did over those never-to-be-enough admired Antients. It is impossible to say when Mrs. *Hippocrene* would have put a Stop to her Harangue, had not *Clio* met with a small *Disgratia*. That young Lady, observing with envious Eyes, that her Sister *Calliope* filled her Spoon oftener than herself, contrived to revenge the Insult, by over-turning the
Tripod,

Tripod, which stood as the Representative of a Table. This Accident very much disconcerted Mrs. *Hippocrene*; for the shock was so sudden, that she had not Time to save her own *Ambrosial Pot.* She had, however, Presence of Mind enough to correct the little Muse, and to endeavour to preserve the Remains of her Morning high-flavoured Draught. *Emily* took Advantage of the Confusion they were all in, and withdrew.

When Mr *Hippocrene* returned from *London* in the Evening, *Emily* communicated to him Mrs. *Easy*'s Proposal, which he did not at first seem to relish; but when she gave a broad Hint that she would, in case of his making Objections to it, and refusing his Consent, chuse another Guardian, he began to demur, and told her he wou'd consider about it. He then left her, and went in Search of his Help-mate, whom he found in her Bower, lolling in a careless Posture, with a Collection of Manuscript Pastorals in her Hand, composed by herself, some Parts of which she repeated in the most emphatic, ecstatic Manner. She was, in short, so enraptur'd with the Spinnings of her own

Brain, that her Spouse entered the Bower unperceived. When he waked her from her Raptures, and told her the Reason of his Intrusion, she cried out, Lard, Mr *Hippocrene*, you cou'd not have pitched upon a more unlucky Hour in the whole Four-and-twenty. I was just fallen into the most delicious Fit of musing on my dear Nosegay here. Sure it is quite a Wilderness of Sweets! And to be interrupted in such an abrupt Manner, when, perhaps, I may not be so happy again in a whole *Roman Lustre*, is——Well, but Child, said *Hippocrene*, I must have a conference with you. *Emily*, a foolish Girl, wants to leave us, and you know we shall lose a good round Sum if she persists.—I know that, replied his Lady, but 'twill be your own Fault if you let her go. Sure a Guardian has Power over his Ward, or else—Nay but, Child, said he, I believe she can chuse another Guardian, as she threatens to do.——Poo, poo, replied she, marry her to my Brother out of Hand. When once she is married, she will be wiser, I warrant.—But, my Dear, said *Hippocrene*, I am not clear that I can force her to marry him, and if I cou'd, what Advantage will thereby accrue

crue to us, since her Husband then must have her Money?—Why let him, said Mrs *Hippocrene*, and then we shall get rid of him. He has long been a Burden to us. But, indeed, Mr *Hippocrene*, I cannot be disturbed by these sublunary Things. My Ideas were soaring beyond all human Conception, when you put them to Flight, by talking of this trifling Girl.—The Interest of a thousand Pounds, said he, is, in my Opinion, worth thinking about, and is more, I believe, than the sublimest of your Ideas will ever procure.—Mr. *Hippocrene*, said she, with inexpressible Haughtiness, I am astonished at the Meanness of your Behaviour this Evening. You seem to have sprung from the lowest of all Reptiles, if one may form any Judgment by your Style. My Ideas, Sir, I would have you know, are superior, far superior to any you ever were favour'd with; nay, so very low, you are fallen in my Estimation, that I much question if you ever had Ideas of Consequence. Poor, groveling Wretch, to speak so slightly of my excellent Composition! A Composition which shall vie with any one among the Antients, for Chastity of Sentiment, and Smoothness of Versification.

And which will be read and admired, when your paltry Tragedy will only be found in Chandlers Shops, the proper Receptacles of such incoherent, unintelligible Jargon.

Heaven and Earth! cried *Hippocrene*, don't vilify my Piece, a Piece that shall *act* with any in the Universe —Chandlers Shops! Hell and Furies!——but you are a Woman, a poor weak Woman; or, by the immortal Gods, I would make an Example of you—— Chandlers Shops!—No *Man*, replied Mrs *Hippocrene*, wou'd dare to use such false, injurious Expressions. Why, you conceited Creature, do you imagine that your Play will be better received than those of your most admired Predecessors of the Pen have been? Are not the finest Plays that ever were written, found Fault with by Somebody? Do you, alone, expect to escape Censure, you who have huddled together such a Heap of chaotic Rhodomontade? — Woman, Woman, cried *Hippocrene*, how dare you thus inveigh against the most perfect Piece that ever was composed? A Piece which cannot be parallel'd?—Aye, said she, your Piece might have been perfect,

if

if you had inserted what I had sketch'd out for you ——'Sdeath and the Devil, cried he, why you have not the Impudence, I hope, to think of comparing yourself to me! But you'll never be cur'd of your Vanity. You would make yourself a more useful Member of Society, by looking after your Family, and providing Necessaries for them. Your Children are as ragged as Colts, and must be, if their Mother, fancying herself a Genius, is always handling her Pen instead of her Needle, and making Pastorals instead of mending Stockings.

Very fine, Sir, said she, very fine, indeed! And do you really expect me to be so domestic an Animal, such a mere Houshold Drudge as to mend Stockings? No, Sir, you are quite mistaken! I have a Soul which scorns such servile Offices: A Soul, Mr. *Hippocrene*, every way equal to your own. Nay, I think I may venture to say superior. For you have very much degraded yourself in my Eyes, by mentioning such an ignoble Occupation as darning of Stockings to me—to me, who, thank Heaven, have Talents peculiar to myself; which

you,

you, thro' Envy, endeavour to obfuscate, but I shall relumine them with my wonted Vigour.

Hippocrene, during this eloquent Speech, seemed in a profound Reverie, (or what is generally called a *brown Study*) which he fell into by reflecting on the Hints his Lady gave about Faultfinders. A Set of Men he cou'd not think of with Patience. After a short Pause, therefore, he vented his Indignation in the following Manner, having first seized one of the Laths of the Arbor, by way of Weapon, which he brandish'd in the Air:—Yes, by all the Deities, I will defend with my honest Heart's Blood, what my honest Hand has written. Avaunt, ye snarling Critics, ye Merit-crushing Tribe, or by the fiery Arm of the dread Thunderer, I'll dart down swift Destruction on your Heads ——— Just as he had finished this heroic Rhapsody, a large Sow, which had been worried by mischievous Boys, in the adjoining Yard, broke thro' the Paling, ran directly between his Legs, and threw him flat on his Face: The Bard was so astounded by this rough Rencounter, that he lay for some Time
without

without Senfe or Motion; his Spoufe therefore was greatly alarm'd, and fcream'd in fo violent a Manner for Help, that the whole Family was quickly affembled, and, among the reft, the Owner of the Beaft, who from a third Ground had beheld the Accident. The Landlord, the Landlady and Mifs *Wilr*, all, at once, demanded the caufe of this fudden Outcry, while the Hog driver prefently turn'd the Creature back again, without ftaying to afk any Queftions, for fear of being indicted, or of having his Beaft pounded for breaking a Fence.

Mrs. *Hippocrene* having, with the Affiftance of her Landlord, who was a Higgler, fet her Hufband upon his Legs again, afked him how he found himfelf, and if the ungovernable Boar had no where perforated his Flefh with his formidable Tufks. A Monfter of a more enormous fize, faid fhe, I never faw, nor do I believe they were common among the *Romans*. *Mark An'ony* indeed might poffibly have had as large a one ferved up to his Table, though I have fome Doubts about it—God blefs my Soul, Madam, faid the Higgler, this was no Boar,

Boar, but a Sow juſt ready to farrow, whom the Boys have been plaguing this Hour, an it is well if it doant make her ſlip her Pigs.—Why ſure, replied Mrs *Hippocrene*, I know a Boar from a Sow when I ſee it, I am not arrived to theſe Years, a Mother of Children and the Matron of a Family, without perfectly comprehending the Difference betwixt Male and Female. The Countryman, who thought he was full as well acquainted with the Difference of Sexes as the Lady, was going to reply, when his Wife, fearing he might expreſs himſelf too coarſely, pulled him by the Arm, and cried, Hold your Tongue, *Robin*, you talk like a Fool, and you know I always tell you ſo: You have affronted Madam already, who for *ſartin* has more *Learnin* than we; therefore go about your Buſineſs, and let me hear no more of you. The poor Fellow ſneaked off at this Reprimand, but as he went, beſtowed a few hearty Curſes on all Women who pretend to be more knowing than their Huſbands.

Mr. *Hippocrene* was now thoroughly recovered from his Fright, and return'd very patiently to the Houſe, in which, during

during their Evening Repast, Mrs. *Hippocrene* related several wonderful Stories of savage Beasts, which she had collected from several Authors and jumbled together, to the no small Amazement of the good Woman of the House who waited on them.

When the Family retired to rest, Mr. *Hippocrene* found a favourable Opportunity to resume the Subject so unluckily begun in the Bower. Mrs *Hippocrene* agreed to *Emily*'s Departure, when her Husband had convinced her that he could, by winking at it, with-hold the Interest of her Money, under a Pretence that she went away without his Consent

Next Morning, *Emily*, who was eager to quit a Family so very disagreeable to her, again mentioned her Intentions to Mr. *Hippocrene*, who told her he could never approve of them, and blamed her Obstinacy, but said she might go or stay just as she pleased, being determined not to bias her one Way or the other, or to interfere with her Affairs.

Emily thought the above Answer of her Guardian was sufficient to countenance her Proceedings, and accordingly waited on Mrs. *Easy* with the News.

Mrs. *Easy* told her she had wrote to a Lady, with whom she was going to spend a Fortnight, in her Behalf, and waited for an Answer, which she hoped to contain a *double* Invitation. *Emily* was highly pleased to hear of her Friend's kind Intentions, and thanked her in the strongest Terms for writing favourably of her. But my Dear, said Mrs. *Easy*, you ought not to go away quite unprovided with Money, you may also want some Trifles which cannot be procured in the Country. I would therefore advise you to tell *Hippocrene* that a Supply of Money is absolutely necessary, as you may stay several Months there. *Emily* said she had a good Stock of Cloaths when Mrs. *Dawson* died, and wanted no Addition, having but just left off her Mourning—But Money, Child, said Mrs. *Easy*, never comes *mal-a-propos*; besides, when you are at a Distance from him, you perhaps may find it difficult to get a Remittance, therefore if I was in your Situation, I would

would try to secure a large Sum before I left him. *Em'y* promised to follow her Advice, and went Home for that Purpose, but could find no Opportunity to consult Mr *Hippocrene*, who was obliged to stay in Town the Remainder of the Week.

Emily remained in a great Suspence till *Saturday* Night. She then received a Message from Mrs *Easy*, to whom she immediately went full of Joy, and was welcomed by her as the Companion of her Journey ——— I have just now, said she, been favoured with an Answer from Mrs *Freelove*, who permits me to carry you with me On *Tuesday* next we are to set out Her Coach brings her Nephew to Town To-morrow, and will take us down And now, continued she, it will not be amiss to give you an Insight into the Character of the Lady you are going to live with

Mrs *Freelove* is near sixty Years of Age. She was very handsome in her youthful days, and may now be called a fine old Gentlewoman. But her *Person* is the last Thing she regards. Family

mily Pride is her grand Foible, which she carries to a great Height, but she is otherwise a good Sort of Woman. You must therefore, always pay her vast Respect, never presume to contradict her; but be very submissive to her Will; she will then, I dare say, handsomely provide for you. *Emily* promised to follow her Directions, and said, I hope, Madam, you will be so obliging as to make me acquainted with every little Particularity in this Lady's Disposition, that I may know how to gain her good Opinion.—We shall have Time enough, replied Mrs. *Easy*, to enquire more minutely into her Character upon the Road. You have nothing to do but to prepare the *Hippocrenes* for your Journey, and be ready yourself to go with me to *London* on *Monday* Morning, for the Coach will call for us at my Lodging in Town; to which your Things shall be carried from your Guardian's.

Emily, at her Return Home from the above Visit, found Mr. *Hippocrene* in a violent Heat, being just arrived from his Shop, and thoroughly fatigued with so long a Walk. The Information she gave

gave him, which ended with a Demand of Money, did not contribute to allay it, for he told her, with some Vehemence, that she had received all the Money he could spare, to defray the Expences of her Mourning, that he was certain she could not so soon want Cloaths, &c. That he had not finger'd her Half-year's Interest, and therefore would not advance a Shilling. In vain did she endeavour by all the Arts of Persuasion to mollify his Heart; he was deaf to all she could say on that Subject, and carefully avoided her the Remainder of the Evening. *Emily*, in short, could not get at him till the next Day at Dinner, (for his *Sunday* Mornings were always dedicated to Mrs. *Hippocrene* and his Tragedy in the Bower) she then told him, that Mrs. *Easy* had hired a Coach to carry them to Town the next Morning, and desired to know when he would be at his Shop, that she might send for her Things. He coolly replied, that he could not pretend to give an Account of his Time to *her* and Mrs. *Easy*, and that he should give himself no Trouble about her Things.

No indeed, I think not truly, said Mrs *Hippocrene*, when a young Person withdraws herself from her Guardian's Protection, he must act with the most erroneous Absurdity, if he gives up any Thing in his Possession. I am sure I would not part with the least Trifle, nor do I believe Mr. *Hippocrene* will, nay, I question whether he can give up any Thing with Safety. You must not think, Miss *Willis*, that you have People of no Knowledge to deal with Mr. *Hippocrene* is very capable of acting properly on every Occasion, and as for me, I have long been esteemed particularly fortunate in being favoured with the extraordinary Gift of Penetration and Science, even to so infinite a Degree, as never to have been guilty of a weak Action; therefore, Miss, expect nothing from us, we know better than to —— Here the Bard interrupted his loquacious Spouse, for fear she might discover what both Interest and Inclination prompted him to conceal, and peevishly said, Come, come, come we have had enough of one Subject, let us talk of something else. Methinks, *Hannah*, this Tripe wants Seasoning, or something. I don't much like it.—This unlucky

Reflection

Reflection on Mrs. *Hippocrene*'s Negligence in Cookery, rouzed her fiercest Passions: With a Face therefore crimson'd with Anger, and Eyes flashing Indignation, she thus replied:—Well, Sir, and if you don't like it, pray who is to bear the Blame but yourself, for providing such beggarly Nutriment for your Family?—Why the Devil's in the Woman, I believe, said he, I only observed it wanted Seasoning.—Don't tell me of Seasoning, said she, do you think I don't know how to boil a little Tripe without your Direction? I wou'd have you to know, Sir, that I would not give Place to that notable Matron *Andromache* herself, if she was now living, in Culinary Acquisitions, but you're a poor sneaking, miserable wretch. What! is it not enough to be compelled to masticate and concoct such filthy Diet, but I must be told I have not Skill enough to dress it? Oh! I shall certainly faint!—Here, *Clio*, go and bring down the Bottle which stands by my Bed-side.

The tattered Muse immediately obeyed, and while she was on her Errand, her Mamma broke out into the following Soliloquy. Why, why am I so unfortunate as to exist at this Period of Time, a Period when every Person, every Thing is vile, low, gross, and indelicate! Or why, being thus shockingly misplaced, am I endued with such superior, such towering Sensations! Am I, who could subsist on the purest Æther, or sip with Extacy the Liquor of the Gods, formed to imbibe the Entrails of a Cow? perhaps a distempered Cow? Forbid it, all ye heavenly Powers!——— I can endure no more.———Just as she pronounced the last Word, *Clio* returned with a Quart Bottle of Brandy, which her Mamma applied hastily to her Mouth. Whilst she was comforting herself with that Care-dispelling Cordial, the Bard declared his Approbation of her Soliloquy, which, said he, with some slight Alterations in the Diction, and a few grammatical Amendments, I can make a high-finish'd Thing.

Emily, finding no Opportunity to turn the Conversation on her own Affairs, left the Bard and his Wife to their Heroics, and slipt away to Mrs. *Easy*.

When

When she was gone, *Hippocrene* renewed his Endeavours to prevail on his Spouse to *let* the *Girl go off* without a Fuss, and after much Elocution, and many Arguments, at length succeeded; chiefly by assuring her, that they should be Gainers by her Departure.

About an Hour before the Family went to *roost*, *Emily* returned, and told Mrs. *Hippocrene* that she would take Leave of her then, as the Coach might perhaps call very early in the Morning. Mrs. *Hippocrene* coldly replied, I wish you a pleasant Journey; and after having pronounced very theatrically this laconic Sentence, The good Gods grant us a good Night, stalk'd away with a majestick Air to her *Dormitory*.

The Reader will, undoubtedly, wonder, that a Lady endowed with such a Volubility of Tongue, should be able to check it so much just at the Parting-Scene. I must therefore inform him, or her, that she had actually composed a long, florid Speech for the Occasion, and would have added to it the Graces of Pronunciation, had not her considerate

siderate Husband intreated her in the melting Moments of Reconcilement, to suppress it, for fear any ill Consequences should arise from the Repetition of it.

When Mrs. *Hippocrene* was withdrawn, *Emily* addressed herself to her Guardian thus. I hope, Sir, you will be at your House To-morrow at Four o'Clock, because I intend to call and pack up my Things. If you are not there, I shall leave a Direction that you may send them to me. I beg the Favour of you to write to me at Mrs. *Freelove*'s, and to remit the Interest of my Money when it is due, by the Hands of Mrs. *Easy*. *Hippocrene*, without making any Answer, instantly turn'd his Back on her, grasp'd his Taper, and followed his Lady's Footsteps with silent Dignity.

Emily rose early the next Morning with Hopes of seeing her Guardian and his Lady again, being dissatisfied with the Taciturnity of the one, and the Coldness of the other, at their going to Rest; but was forced to get into the Coach without that Consolation, for the

the Gentleman strided away to *London* before she opened her Eyes, and the Lady would not budge from her Pillow.

As Mrs *Easy* had paid off her Lodging at *Turnham-Green*, she was under a Necessity of removing several Boxes and Bundles, which, together with the Servant, sufficiently fill'd the Coach, and prevented the Intrusion of other Passengers, to the great Satisfaction of *Emily*, who rejoiced exceedingly at the Thought of conversing with her Friend without Interruption.

When the Coach was driven from the Door, *Emily* said, I can't help being a little uneasy, Madam, at Mr. *Hippocrene*'s Indifference about my Departure, and wish he assumed it for no other Reason but to prevent my Journey to Mrs. *Freelove*'s, from which I expect to receive so much Pleasure —Don't be alarmed, said Mrs. *Easy*, I rather think he wanted to get rid of you, and am only afraid that he will start Difficulties about the Payment of your Interest, but we shall, I hope, be able to surmount them. I cannot blame your Aversion to him, nor wonder at your Desire to leave the
Family

Family; for, setting aside their Attempts to prey upon you, their Manners must be quite unbearable. But, pray, Miss *Willis*, continued she, is this Guardian of your's a Man of Reputation? I suppose you have heard Mrs. *Dawson*'s Opinion of him.—No, indeed Madam, said *Emily*, Mrs. *Dawson* never mentioned him but as a Cousin of her Husband; but I conclude she approved of his Character, by putting me under his Protection: Though neither he nor his Wife behaved to me during her Life-time, as they have behaved since.—Well, my Dear, said Mrs *Easy*, you must wait with Patience till you are of Age, and then you can demand your Fortune, with the *Interest* too, if he refuses to pay it before.

Mrs. *Easy* arrived at her Lodgings about Noon, and sent *Emily*, after Dinner, with her Maid, to Mr. *Hippocrene*'s for her Things.

It may seem odd, perhaps, to some of my Readers, that Mrs. *Easy* should be so excessively fond of, and uncommonly kind to, a young Girl, whom she had only met with by Chance, in a Travelling

Travelling Machine:—But they will cease to wonder, when I tell them the Motives of her Conduct.

Mrs *Easy* was, at first Sight, highly pleas'd with *Emily*; and after conversing with her a little, wished to be better acquainted with her, but had no Intention to take her from her Guardian till she had heard her story, which excited her Pity, and made her recollect that Mr. *Dawson* was a Clerk under *her* Husband, and often mentioned by him with Applause, and that his supposed Niece bore the Character of a very agreeable, modest Girl.——So much, by Way of Digression, to clear Mrs *Easy* from the Imputation of thoughtless Good-nature.

When *Emily* arrived at her Guardian's, and desired to speak with him, a dirty, ill-looking Female, frightfully featur'd, with a cadaverous Complexion, yell'd out, *Master's not at home, went to's Country-place an Hour agone.*—— *Emily* then asked her, if she might take away her Boxes.——Yes, yes, replied the Maid, I have no Orders to hinder you. She then went up Stairs, secured
all

all her Cloaths,, and returned with them to Mrs. *Easy*

Next Morning, about Seven o'Clock, they set out for *Northamptonshire*, in Mrs. *Freelove*'s Coach, and came to the End of an agreeable Journey, the Day following, just before Dinner-Time. — As soon as they enter'd the Court-yard, *Emily* was struck with the *Gothic* Magnificence of a large Mansion-house, and began to doubt whether she could give Satisfaction to the venerable Inhabitant of it. Mrs. *Easy* soon discovered her Uneasiness, and endeavoured to remove her Diffidence: I assure you, said she, that your modest Behaviour will very much recommend you to my Friend's Esteem.

Mrs. *Freelove* received Mrs. *Easy* in her best Parlour, with the highest Politeness, (tho' every Word and Action plainly shewed how much she thought herself superior to her) and then said, turning to *Emily*, Is this the Person you mention'd, *Easy*? She looks very young —but I like her the better for that—— I chuse to have young People about me. There's an Alacrity, a Readiness in them,

them, if they are of an obliging Dispofition, which is vastly preferable to the lingering of Age. Oh, *Easy*, what would you and I give to be as young and as blooming as this Girl!—Why, I don't know, Madam, said Mrs. *Easy*, whether the youthful Part of Life is to be envied. I am apt to believe that a healthy Middle-age, when the Passions begin to subside, is more substantially happy, than that Period in which the Warmth of our Inclinations often drives us to commit Exravagancies, that give great Uneasiness to ourselves and to those about us.—Aye, aye, said Mrs. *Freelove* smiling, you moralize finely, but your young Friend here, I fancy, will not be of your Opinion, tho' she looks very mild and sensible. Do you think, Child, continued she to *Emily*, you can like to live cloyster'd up with an old Woman? Though I shall not be severe, if you are prudent and please me.

Emily blushed and curtsied, and assured her, that she would endeavour to make herself as useful as she could. Very well, said Mrs. *Freelove*, I hope we shall agree, for I am already prepossessed

possessed in your Favour: You have a very good, ingenuous Countenance: But you will not always be alone with me. I have a Niece, Lady *Caroline*, who sometimes stays a Month or two with me, and I will recommend you to her Notice, if you don't behave amiss. *Emily* again assured her, that she would study to deserve her Favours, and the Conversation then turn'd on indifferent Subjects.

As soon as *Emily* found herself in private with her Friend Mrs. *Easy*, she thanked her repeatedly, for introducing her to *Fairly-Manor*. I am quite charm'd with Mrs. *Freelove*, said she to her; she is very affable and kind to me, and I am sure I can be happy with her. But who is this Lady *Caroline* ?—Mrs. *Freelove*'s eldest Sister, replied Mrs. *Easy*, was married to an Earl, and died young, but left a Son and Daughter, of whom their Aunt is very fond. As they were always idolized by their Father, they have had a careless Education, and are apt to be too much enslaved by their Passions. Lord *B——* is rather an insipid, than a vicious Character. Lady *Caroline* is a fine Girl, but seems to be so conscious of her personal Charms, that there is no Occasion to put her in mind of them. I wou'd advise you, therefore, my dear *Emily*, to pay your Court to *her*, as she has a great Influence over her Aunt. Mrs. *Freelove* has, also, a Nephew of her Husband's, who visits her sometimes, a young Baronet. He is a very agreeable Gentleman, but not without the Foibles which generally stick close to Youth, Rank and Fortune. Be upon your Guard, therefore, and remember, that if you suffer either of these Gentlemen to take Liberties with you, for your Situation with Mrs *Freelove*, and your engaging Appearance, may possibly induce them to treat you with Familiarity; remember, I say, that a Dismission from the Family, with the Loss of Reputation, must inevitably follow. Women, now-a-days, seldom make their Fortunes by Men, especially Men of Fashion, who are generally educated in too licentious a Manner to have any just Notions of Virtue. Nay, if they should happen to esteem it, and wish to reward it, the Family is so incensed, very often, at the insolent Creature who wants to be *one* of *them*, that they do every Thing in their Power to hinder the Alliance; and if they fail of Success, never rest till they have, by blackening her Character, made her so odious, in the Eyes of her Admirer, that he grows to hate her, and look upon her as the Author of his Ruin. Avoid therefore, my dear Girl, an Intimacy with Men in so high a Sphere; and rather chuse a Companion among your Equals; in point of Rank and Circumstances, I mean; but let his Mind and Behaviour give Place to none. Then will his Company be sought after, and esteemed by every body. I have spent the greatest Part of my Life among People of Distinction: I have studied their Manners, and know they are the easiest People to live with, if one has but the Art to manage them.—No Body, I believe, my dear *Emily*, is happier than I am, yet I never placed my Felicity in *Person* or *Dress*, but in conforming to the Taste and Humour of Persons I chanced to be with. This pliant Disposition has always procured me a welcome Reception every where, and the Characters, I have met with, have afforded me such a Variety of Amusement, that Time has never been a Burden to me

With

With this fort of Chat did Mrs *Eafy* and *Emily* fill up the Hours they enjoyed by themfelves. *Emily* made herfelf every Day more and more agreeable to Mrs. *Freelove*, who frequently told Mrs. *Eafy* how much fhe was obliged to her for recommending fo ufeful a Companion.

Mrs *Freelove*, having received from Mrs. *Eafy*, a full Account of *Emily*'s Affairs, advifed her to write to her Guardian about the Payment of her Money. *Emily* wrote accordingly, but could obtain no Anfwer from the Bard: His Silence, however, did not give her much Uneafinefs, as fhe was thoroughly fatisfied with her Situation, which became ftill more pleafing, as Mrs. *Freelove* was luckily fond of Mufick, a Science in which fhe herfelf excelled, and employed her an Hour or two every Day at the Harpfichord. So that by fometimes playing and finging, fometimes by reading, drawing, airing in the Coach, and doing fine Needle-work, the Hours were filled up agreeably, *and varied Life ftole unperceived away.*

Mrs. *Eafy*, after ftaying a Week longer at *Fairly Manor* than fhe intended, took

Leave of it, in order to prepare for a journey into *Northumberland*, with a Family of her Acquaintance. When she embraced *Emily* at parting, she told her how to direct to her, and received a Letter from her for Mr. *Hippocrene*, which she promised to deliver to him, as she was obliged to be a Week in Town, before she set out to the *North*.

Poor *Emily*, who now looked upon Mrs *Eafy* as the best Friend she had in the World, could not see her depart without shedding Tears plentifully, and begging to hear from her by every Opportunity. Mrs *Freelove* very much commended her for shewing so much Esteem for the *good Eafy* (that was her Expression) and, to alleviate her Anxiety, introduced her, as her Companion, to several genteel Families, whom she visited, in the Neighbourhood.

END of the FIRST BOOK.

EMILY

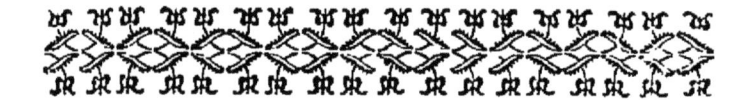

EMILY WILLIS:

OR, THE

HISTORY

OF A

NATURAL DAUGHTER.

BOOK II.

*E*MILY spent two Months (during which she received many Letters from her *Friend*, but not a Line from her *Guardian*) in this agreeable Manner, high in her Lady's Esteem, and much caressed by the neighbouring Gentry of both Sexes —The Current of her Happiness was then interrupted by a Series of cross Incidents, with which the Reader shall, in due Time, be acquainted.

One Morning as she was amusing herself with her Pen, she was informed of the Arrival of Lord *B——*, and Lady *Caroline*; she was likewise told, that Mrs *Freelove* expected her in the Parlour directly. She therefore left her 'Scrutore, and hastened to her Benefactress, who presented her to Lady *Caroline, as a young Person for whom she had some Regard.* Lady *Caroline* received her with great Politeness, but viewed her at the same Time with a Kind of envious Dislike. Lord *B——* beheld her with more favourable Eyes, for, as he had formed no advantageous Idea of his Aunt's Companion, he was surprized to see her enter the Room with so much easy Dignity, and behave with so much graceful Simplicity He was, in short, quite enchanted, and thought her the finest Creature he had ever seen.

Lady *Caroline* was about eighteen, of the middle Size, and tolerably well shaped Her Features were small, and so regular, that she would have been reckoned a Beauty, had not her Complexion been as pale as Ashes Lord *B——* was neither handsome nor ugly, neither

neither foolish nor wise, neither good-humour'd nor ill-humoured —A very middling Character —With these two young Visitors, *Emily* spent a great Part of her Time, and diligently studied to gain their Esteem, rather out of Regard to Mrs. *Freelove*, than from any Inclination to *them*. But she soon found, though she had but little Skill in the Language of the Eyes, that the Esteem of both was not to be obtained. His Lordship seem'd to place his whole Happiness in her Company, and endeavoured to make himself agreeable to her with uncommon Assiduity.—— Lady *Caroline* was too much taken up with her *sweet Self*, to observe what passed between her Brother and *Emily*— As for Mrs *Freelove*, she loved the Company of young People, being naturally of a chearful Disposition, and was pleased with the Good-humour of those about her, not having the least Apprehension that her Nephew would so far demean himself as to think of looking on a Girl, whom she had, from a charitable Motive, made her Companion.

Mrs. *Freelove*, tho' she allowed *Emily* to be a handsome and an accomplished Girl, would have shuddered at the Thought of calling her *Niece:* Nor had his Lordship any Intention to confer that Title on her, having a Touch of his Aunt's Disposition, which could not bear the Sound of Degradation. As he was just of Age, and had thereby a small independent Fortune, he only proposed to make the best Use he could of those cogent Arguments, Bribery and Adulation, in order to gain her for a Mistress.

Emily, who grew every Day more clear-sighted, gave him no Opportunity to speak to her alone, but constantly avoided him, unless he was with his Aunt or his Sister. He waited some Time impatiently, but, finding she would never let him have a *private Audience*, at length determined to try what Effect an Epistle would have on her. He therefore penned one without Delay, and conveyed it secretly into her Work-basket: It was filled with a great many extravagant Professions, such as *Vows of eternal Love*, &c. but the Burden of it was, a *genteel Settlement*.

Emily,

Emily, when she found the Letter, open'd it eagerly, as she didn't know from whom it came. But redden'd with Indignation to think that his Lordship had so mean an Opinion of her. She committed it immediately to the Flames, and resolved to take no Notice of it to any body, but treated the Author of it with less Familiarity afterwards, and constantly shunn'd him, when she cou'd, without being observed by Mrs. *Freelove* This Alteration in her Behaviour, he, who watched her every Motion, soon perceived, but his Desire to know her Sentiments was only thereby increased. He waited a great while for an Opportunity to speak to her alone, and at last hit upon a Scheme which succeeded as he wish'd.

One Morning before his Aunt was stirring, he ventured to knock softly at *Emily*'s Chamber-door, as he knew she was an early Riser. *Emily* being up and dressed, ran hastily to turn the Key, thinking to receive a visit from Lady *Caroline*, who sometimes condescended to honour her Apartment so far. She was just going to express her Surprize at seeing her Ladyship so early, when the

Appearance of my Lord struck her dumb, and filled her with Confusion. As she was quite unprepared for such a Visitor, she could not immediately tell how to receive him; but when she recollected the Insolence of his Behaviour, and consider'd the Impropriety of the Time and Place he had chosen to speak to her, her Resentment was rouzed, and she was going to treat him very roughly, when he endeavoured to avert her Anger, by desiring her, in an humble Posture, to hear patiently what he had to say for himself. The Humility, with which he introduced his Request, prevented her from uttering what she had intended, but her Countenance sufficiently shew'd how much she was displeased with his Proceedings. She replied, with some Warmth, Your Lordship has no Business in my Apartment. I therefore beg you would leave it directly. She then offered to shut the Door, but he stopt her Hand, and said, Hear me one Moment—Pray hear me. I have long wished to speak to you in private; I have long waited for an Opportunity, but have never been able to find one; nay I have great Reason to believe, that you have yourself prevented me from—

After

After the Letter you wrote to me, my Lord, interrupted *Emily*, with a difdainful look, you ought not to expect any other Behaviour from me. While I am honoured with your Aunt's Protection, tho' I am inferior to your Lordship in Point of Rank and Fortune, I am intitled to a different Treatment, especially from her own Family. *Emily* spoke these Words with a sharp Accent, and hindered him from making any Reply, by suddenly shutting the Door

Lord B—— was forced to retreat without carrying his Point. He was thoroughly vext at his *Repulse*, but more than ever delighted with the fair *Repeller*. He had, like most young Noblemen, no contemptible Opinion of himself; and therefore thought that his intended Mistress was possessed of uncommon Virtue, because she had resisted so handsome a Fellow, with so handsome a Settlement. In short, he ruminated on this Affair, with unusual Seriousness, and, at length, began to fancy that he should run no very great Risque, by taking *Emily* for a Wife, since she was not to be caught by any Lure but Matrimony. He was charm'd with her

Person, and now, for the first Time, believed that her Mind was equal to it. I must, said he, inherit my Father's Estate at his Death, and I can make a tolerable Shift with my present Income till he dies. After this Soliloquy, he resolved to make her a second Offer; an Offer which he imagined would be too advantageous for any Woman to reject.

Two Days glided away before he could put his new Scheme in Execution, (so vigilant was *Emily*) nor would he then have succeeded, had he not had Recourse to the following Stratagem. He ordered his Phaeton to be ready early in the Morning, and told Mrs. *Freelove*, when he took Leave of her, that he should spend the Day abroad: He went however but a little Way from the House, and then alighted, ordering his Servant to carry the Vehicle to the nearest Inn till the Evening, and to wait for him then at one of the Park Gates. When he had given these Orders, he concealed himself behind a little Temple in the Garden, which he knew *Emily* often retired to, when she could enjoy her own Company, but which she had avoided

avoided ever since the Receipt of his *familiar* Epistle. He spent several Hours in fruitless Expectation, and was just going to quit a Post which began to grow very disagreeable, when the Sight of *Emily*, pacing slowly along the verdant Walk which pointed to her favourite Retreat, cheered his drooping Spirits. His Eyes sparkled with Hope, his Heart bounded for Joy, and the wearisome Moments he had passed, were instantly forgotten. So excessive indeed was his Transport, that it would not suffer him to stay till she was seated. He flew to her with the Swiftness of Lightning, and thus accosted her. How fortunate am I, dear Miss *Willis*, to have the Pleasure of meeting with you alone!—*Emily*, who was both surprized and vext at the Appearance of his Lordship, deem'd it most prudent to shew her thorough Aversion to him, by declining to parley, and accordingly turned from him with a Design to make the best of her Way to her *Asylum*, that is, Mrs. *Freelove*'s Apartment, in which she never was under any Apprehensions from his Impertinence. But this Design of her's was no sooner plann'd than frustrated; for his Lordship, being arch enough

enough to comprehend the Meaning of her Looks, seized her Hand, and poured out his Supplications in the following Manner — For Heaven's Sake, Miss *Willis*, hear me attentively. I am not now going to insult you with Proposals, which, I find, with real Satisfaction, are disagreeable to you. Yes, my charming *Emily*, I am convinced of my Error, and will submit to any Thing, to obtain your Pardon. But then you must listen to other Proposals which I have impatiently waited, ever since our last Meeting, to communicate to you   He then told her of his Intention to marry her, and eagerly solicited her Consent to their Union.

If *Emily* was surprized at meeting his Lordship in the Garden, at a Time when she thought he was at a great Distance from it, how much more was she astonished at his new Offer, which he delivered very seriously and with great Earnestness? The Offer, indeed, was of so extraordinary a Nature, that she wisely doubted the Sincerity of it, and, endeavouring to disengage her Hand, thus replied· Pray, my Lord, let me be permitted to leave you.———I am not used
to

to be thus jested with. She spoke these Words with so grave an Air, that he concluded she wanted Faith, and therefore held her fast, and assured her, in the most solemn Manner, that he was in Earnest.—Banish all Distrust, said he, I intend not to deceive you. We will speedily be married: You shall pitch upon the Man you can most confide in, to perform the Ceremony, and you shall invite as many of your Friends as you chuse to be Witnesses to the Performance of it. All I desire, is, that this Scheme may not be divulged, till it is executed. —The plausible Manner in which his Lordship utter'd this Speech, entirely removed *Emily*'s Suspicions about the Dishonourableness of his Intentions, but she was Proof against his Addresses of every Kind, and, without much Hesitation, made the following Reply: I am very much obliged to you, my Lord, for the favourable Opinion you entertain of me, but can, by no Means, think of complying with your Request. Our Situations in Life are widely different, and disproportionate Matches are seldom happy. Besides, my Lord, if I should consent to an Union with *you*, I should be guilty of Ingratitude to one of the

most

most amiable Women in the World; that is, your Aunt, to whose kind Protection and Benevolence all my present Felicity is owing, and to whom, therefore, I would not render myself odious on any Account. Let me then, my Lord, retire, and let me intreat you to think no more of one who is so very much beneath your Notice. For your own, as well as for your good Aunt's Sake, let my Words make an Impression on you At the Conclusion of this Speech, *Emily* rush'd abruptly from him, and ran towards the House. *He* ran too in order to overtake her, supposing that she declined his Proposal through Modesty, and not want of Inclination But the sudden Appearance of Lady *Caroline*, who tript out of another Walk and followed *Emily*'s Steps, obliged him to put a Stop to his Pursuit, and to return unsuccessful to the Park; where he, not a little fretted at his Disappointment, vented his Chagrin, by cursing the haughty Girl, and vowing not to be so baffled another Time.

Emily, tho' she had the good Luck to escape from the impertinent Sollicitations

tions of his Lordship, was, however, not less chagrin'd than himself, as she was fearful that Mrs *Freelove* wou'd find out his particular Attachment to her, and discard her from the Family, to prevent Mischief.

Lord B———— re-attempted several Times to renew the Subject of Love, but *Emily* continually shunn'd a close Conference, and behaved to him with so much distant Civility, that his Pride was at length piqued at her Indifference, and he took Leave of *Fairy-Manor*, tho' not without the greatest Reluctance.

Emily sincerely rejoiced at his Departure, and began to resume her former Vivacity. Soon after the above-mention'd Transactions, Sir *George Freelove* arrived from *London*, with a Design to spend a few Weeks with his Aunt before he went to *Bath*. As this Gentleman will have a considerable Share in the subsequent Part of this History, the Reader may not, perhaps, be displeased with a Description of his personal and mental Accomplishments.

Sir

Sir *George Freelove* was about Three-and-twenty, and exceeding handsome; well-featur'd, well-complexion'd, and well-made; strong without Awkwardness, and delicate without Effeminacy, neither a Fribble nor a Bruiser. His Limbs were elegantly proportioned, and the *Fine Gentleman* was conspicuous in all his Motions. As he had not injured his Constitution by heedlesly pursuing the Vices in Vogue, the Glow of Health, that best Vermillion, overspreaded his Face, which received new Lustre from a Pair of well-set Eyes. Such was his outward Form, nor was his Mind less amiable. He had a remarkable share of good Sense, which was greatly improved by Reading and Conversation. He was benevolent and generous, affable and discreet. And, in the Management of an Estate of about 2000*l per Annum*, judiciously avoided the two Rocks of Parsimony and Profusion. With all these good Qualities he had but one Failing—an invincible Aversion to Matrimony.

Sir *George* arrived about Eight in the Evening, and found Mrs *Freelove* in a little Room in the Garden, called the Grotto,

Grotto, (because it was incrusted with Shell-work) listening to *Emily*, who was playing one of *Handel*'s Concertos on a fine Silver-ton'd Harpsichord. Sir *George* complimented his Aunt on her *musical* Taste; said he was extravagantly fond of *Handel*'s Compositions, and begged that the *harmonious* Entertainment might not be interrupted. He was attending, with Looks of Rapture, to *Emily*'s Face and Finger, when Lady *Caroline* flounc'd into the Grotto, and cried, Dear Sir *George*, you are the welcomest Creature alive. How long have you been here? Lard, you can't think how miserable I wanted Company.—I can hardly think so, Lady *Caroline*, said Sir *George*, when you have it in your Power to be thus entertained.—Aye, what you are fond of Music, I think, replied she carelessly, and looking as if she wish'd that *Emily* would leave the *Instrument*, who, fancying that Conversation might now be more agreeable, rose from her Seat as soon as she had finished the *Piece*: But Sir *George* gently replaced her in it, and thus addressed his Aunt.—I hope, Madam, you will permit this Lady to satisfy me whether the Melody and Execution of her Voice are

are equal to the well-temper'd Agility of her Fingers.—You will very foon, replied Mrs *Freelove*, have an Opportunity to form a Judgment of both together; for *Emily* is a very good Girl, and has none of thofe ridiculous Affectations fo common among thofe who want a great deal of preffing. She never anfwers you with an Oh, Dear, I am exceffively hoarfe To-day, and quite low-fpirited, nor makes other Excufes, equally frivolous, continually made ufe of by fine Singers, and the numerous Tribe of wou'd-be fine ones, who only copy their Defects.—*Emily* thank'd Mrs. *Freelove* for her Compliment, and immediately pitched upon her favourite Air, *Let me wand'r not unfeen.* Though fhe fung with Diffidence, the Sweetnefs and Clearnefs of her Voice, and her elegant Manner, quite inchanted Sir *George*, who took great Notice of her Performance, and lavifhed fo many Encomiums on her, that her Cheeks glowed. Lady *Caroline* redden'd with Envy, and endeavoured to change the Converfation. Lard, faid fhe, to Mrs. *Freelove*, this little Cabin is fo hot, Madam, I wonder you are not fuffocated. Come, Sir *George*, what fay you to to a Turn in the Park? My Aunt's *Chinese* Temple is just finished. I'll take you to it, for I believe she is not disposed to make use of her Feet. As Mrs. *Freelove* made no Objection to her Niece's Proposal, Sir *George* was forced to comply with it. But, before he offered his Service to Lady *Caroline*, said to *Emily*, Shan't we have the Pleasure of your Company, Madam?—O no, said Lady *Caroline*, hastily, *Emily* never leaves my Aunt.—Yes, yes, replied Mrs. *Freelove*, *Emily* shall walk with you if she pleases, she has been all Day at her Work and her Music, and too much Sedentariness is not good for young Folks. Go, Child, go and divert yourself with them, said she to *Emily*, a little Exercise, and Change of Scenes, will make you come again with more Spirit to your Harpsichord and your Needle.—*Emily* curtsied Consent, and waited on Sir *George* and Lady *Caroline* to take a View of the new-erected Summer-house, to the no small Satisfaction of the former, and no small Uneasiness of the latter, who talked, however, all the Way as fast as she possibly could, on a hundred and fifty insignificant Subjects, in order to hinder her

from

from speaking, rather than to entertain her Cousin.

Emily, having been accustomed to her Ladyship's insolent Manner of behaving to Inferiors, shewed not the least Appearance of Dislike, but behaved with the greatest Respect to them both. Sir *George* was quite charmed with her, and said and did every Thing to engage her Attention in his Favour. He was, indeed, at first ignorant of *Emily*'s Situation in the Family, and thought she had been the Daughter of some Friend of his Aunt's, who was only on a Visit. But Lady *Caroline* soon undeceived him; being thoroughly piqued at her Aunt's sending *Emily* with them, and still more at the Civilities he shewed her, which she imputed to his not knowing that she was his Aunt's Companion, and not to any particular Merit in *her*, whom she looked upon as one as much inferior to her in Person and Accomplishments, as she was in Birth and Fortune.

Emily soon discovered that her Company was by no Means agreeable to Lady *Caroline*, and therefore very prudently framed an Excuse to Mrs. *Freelove*,
which

which gave her Ladyship an Opportunity to inform Sir *George*, more particularly, what a low, obscure Creature her Aunt had picked up to make a Gentlewoman of. Sir *George* took the Hint, and determined, for *Emily*'s Sake, to be upon his Guard. Luckily for him, when they returned to the House, Lady *Caroline* found a Letter from the Earl her Father, which requested her to set out for *London* as soon as possible, as he had something of great Importance to communicate to her. Sir *George inwardly* rejoiced at this Summons, which her Ladyship received with the utmost Indifference. Mrs. *Freelove*, who really loved her Niece, though she was not blind to her Failings, was loth to part with her, and made her promise to return as soon as the Earl would give her Leave.

When Sir *George* and *Emily* were left alone with Mrs. *Freelove*, they began to delight in each other's Company, and had frequent Opportunities of being together; for, tho' *Emily* was very much taken up with her Benefactress, she had a great many Hours at her own Disposal, which Love taught her how to make

make the most of. For Sir *George*, by his unwearied Assiduity, had made such an Impression on her innocent Heart, that she forwarded his Designs against it, without knowing she did so. I have already said, that his Manners were very engaging, he render'd them still more so, by all the Arts in his Power. And made it his whole Study to please a Girl whose personal Charms had fired him with a Passion which he determined to gratify at all Events, and which was considerably heighten'd when he reflected on her Modesty, good Sense, and many amiable Accomplishments. For our young Knight was not one of those superficial Gallants who are captivated, merely, by a regular *Set of Features*, and a fine *Complexion*, which soon grow *familiar to the Lover*, and, when once familiar, soon fade, and lose the Power of Attraction. No, he loved *Emily* with redoubled Ardour, because he thought she *tower'd above her Sex*, by *inward Greatness, and unaffected Wisdom*. In short, he looked upon her as one formed to make him compleatly blest, and imagined that he shou'd easily gain her Affections, if he could, by any Means.

make

make himself instrumental to her Happiness.

A neighbouring Lady's Mother, who came to pass a few Weeks with her, and who was very intimately acquainted with Mrs. *Freelove*, greatly contributed to facilitate Sir *George*'s Intentions. For, as she and Mrs *Freelove* spent several Hours every Day together, Sir *George* and *Emily* were frequently left to a *Tête-a-Tête*, by themselves.

Sir *George* was a Man too well versed in the Art of Intriguing, not to improve all those lucky Moments to the best Advantage. He studied her Taste in every Thing, and contrived to gratify it. He strove to procure the greatest Variety of Entertainment for her with the most indefatigable Diligence, but took Care not to let the *Lover* appear. He scarcely bestowed a Compliment on her, nay, he would often differ from her in Opinion, but always managed the Debates he had with her so cunningly, that she herself at last seemed to have the best of the Argument. By this wily Behaviour, Sir *George* flattered her Vanity (for where is the Woman whose Vanity would not have been flattered in such a Situation?) and raised a strange Tumult in her tender Bosom. As she was thus followed, thus flattered, thus pleased, by a Man every Way agreeable, she very soon felt Emotions in his Favour, and soon began to prefer him to all his Sex. These Emotions she could not conceal from a Lover of his Penetration. He saw them with Transport, and from the Moment he saw them, determined to put his Design in Execution.

As she was sitting one Day in a musing Posture, upon a Bench in the Garden, with a *Paradise Lost* in her Hand, (with which she had been entertaining her Benefactress, who left her there on hearing of Mrs. *Parker*'s Arrival) Sir *George* accosted her, and, taking the Book from her, asked what Part of that delightful Poem had thrown her into such a *Reverie?* I have just been reading, she replied, *Eve*'s Speech upon her waking from a frightful Dream, which I think is as finely fancied as any other in the whole Poem.—I am entirely of your Opinion, Miss *Willis*, said the Baronet, how great must be the Happiness of that Man, who is possessed of so charming a Companion!—Why I doubt not, said she, smiling, but there are a great many happy Couples in the World.—As to *Couples*, replied he, I can't tell, for by that word we generally mean *wedded Pairs*, and among *them*, I am afraid, Happiness is rarely found —How so, Sir *George?* said *Emily*.— Because, Madam, said he, when People are tied to each other for Life, there is commonly some End to be answered, quite different from that which ought to be the true one for their coming together. Are not Fortunes and Titles the principal Motives to Marriage? And is not poor Love kick'd out of Doors, or what is worse, never thought of by the mercenary Parties, who, if they can but make a blazing Figure *abroad*, care not in the least whether they are happy or wretched, whether they live like Angels or Devils at *Home?*—But certainly, said *Emily*, there are numbers happy who marry only for Love—No really, replied Sir *George*, not many, I believe; and those who happen to be so singular, are commonly left to starve, by their kind Relations, or else grow the Jest of their Acquaintance, and then, you know, they are likely to be soon disagreeable

greeable to each other.—I find then, said *Emily*, you have no Opinion of Love-Matches——I have no Opinion of any Matches at all, replied he, but I have the highest Idea of Love, Madam, that can possibly be conceived. Love refines the Senses, harmonizes the Passions, and makes Life bearable, which, otherwise, would be very burdensome. 'Tis indeed

The Cordial Drop Heav'n in our Cup has thrown,
To make the nauseous Draught of Life go down.

But then I suppose, said *Emily*, you would confine this Cordial to your own Sex, for a Woman you know is reckoned very immodest, if not guilty of a heinous Offence, if she avows a Passion for a Man who has no Intention to marry her.—There I differ from you, replied Sir *George*, I would not give a Pinch of Snuff for the finest Woman in the Universe, if she had not a violent Propensity to this amiable, this laudable Passion. Was *Eve*, Madam, immodest, or guilty of a heinous Offence, because she doated on *Adam*, tho' not married

married to him?—There was no Marriage Ceremony to be performed, said *Emily*, when the happy Pair flourished, neither was there any Occasion for such a Ceremony, because they were the first Pair.—Well, and don't you think, replied Sir *George*, that a Man and a Woman may live happily together now without such a Ceremony, which Priests invented, in order to make themselves of Consequence, and to usurp an Authority over us, to which they have no legal Right? For be assured, Miss *Willis*, that there is no Pleasure in this World without Liberty. You are happy in this Garden, you enjoy all its Beauties, and could stay in it contentedly for several Hours, because you know you can quit it whenever you have a Mind, but if you knew that all the Doors were locked, and that you had no Prospect of a speedy Release, you would soon lose all your Relish for it, impatiently long to have it in your Power either to go or stay, and be very uneasy till you found you were unconfined. And if I could ever bring myself to bear the Marriage Yoke, I should not think myself so much indebted to a

Lady for a Tenderness which is inforced by Duty.

I don't imagine, said *Emily*, that any Man can be pleased with a Woman, unless he is satisfied that she chose him merely from Inclination, without having any mercenary Views; too many of my Sex, are, I am afraid, sway'd in the Choice of a Husband by Splendor, and a Desire of Independency, yet, I am willing to hope, there are some generous Women who give their Hands and Hearts together.—There may be a few such generous Women, replied Sir *George*, but how long do the *fondest* Couples doat? Two or three Months, perhaps——No more. After those are past they generally hate each other with as much Heartiness as they loved before. Take my Word for it, Miss *Willis*, Love, and Love alone, can make us truly happy. Love, voluntary Love, which has nothing to do with Duty and Obedience. I am going to talk very freely to you, Miss *Willis*, but don't be angry. I, at this Moment, (said he, looking at her in a very particular Manner) love with the truest, tenderest Passion, the most amiable Woman in the

the World, and I must be ever miserable if she does not discover and return my Love. I would however give her up this Moment, if I thought she would not yield on softer Terms than those for which you have been so strong an Advocate.

Emily colour'd excessively at the Conclusion of this Speech, which Sir *George* uttered in so peculiar a Manner, that she could not possibly be ignorant for whom it was intended. She began to be alarmed, and afraid to trust herself with so subtle an Arguer, on so delicate a Subject.—I find, Sir *George*, said she, after a short, but confused Pause, you and I are not likely to be of the same Opinion, therefore, if you please, we will part while we are Friends.—I hope, replied he, that Miss *Willis* will always be a Friend to the Man who is thoroughly sensible of, and pays the highest Regard to, her uncommon Merit, and that she will, one Day, pity, at least, a Passion she seems at present not inclined to encourage. *Emily* scarce heard the last Words of this Sentence, so greatly were her Spirits agitated, by the Particularity of Sir *George*'s Behaviour, for he he had kissed her Hand, and press'd it between his own. He looked at her at the same Time with such Tenderness, that she was afraid of staying with him any longer. She therefore hastily withdrew her Hand, told him it was Time for her to return to Mrs *Freelove*, and shot away from him with the Swiftness of a frighted Fawn. Sir *George* made no Attempt to stop her Flight. He was too well versed in the Arts of Gallantry, not to perceive that *Emily* liked him as well as he liked her, and was charmed with the Confusion he had caused in her. But as he believed her to be perfectly modest, he did not care to push Matters too far at first. As I have given her, said he, a few Hints about my Sentiments, that she may not expect I shou'd ever think of marrying her, I have nothing to do now, but to improve the Inclination, she, I am certain, has conceived for me, 'till Love becomes too powerful for Reflection, *then* I shall be sure of her.

While he was thus pluming himself on the Success of his first Attack, poor *Emily* hastened to the House in a far different State of Mind. She had for
some

some Time loved Sir *George*, though she did not know it; but this last Conversation open'd her Eyes, and convinced her of two very important Truths, *viz.* that he was the most agreeable Man she had ever beheld, and that he was endeavouring to gain her for a Mistress. She sighed, when she reflected on what he had been saying to her, but could not compose herself enough to reason about it. When she went to Mis *Freelove*'s Apartment, she found her alone, for Mis *Parker* was just gone before she enter'd. She sat down to the Harpsichord, in order to try if Music could relieve her from the Pain of thinking; but as soon as she had struck the Keys, Sir *George* entered the Room, planted himself over-against her, and fixed his Eyes so meaningly upon her, that she was utterly disconcerted, turned pale, rose from her Seat, and made an Effort to leave the Room. Mis *Freelove* and Sir *George* were both alarmed at the sudden Change in her, including she was very much indisposed. The former said, *Emily*, Child, what's the Matter? The latter flew after her, and, taking hold of her Hand, cried, Where are you going, Mis *Wilis?* You seem to be extremely

tremely ill For God's Sake, sit down, and let me fetch some reviving Cordial. —you frighten me to Death—I cannot bear to see you in this Condition. This Speech he uttered in so low a Voice, that his Aunt could not hear it, but *Emily* lost not a Word of it; but it only increas'd her Disorder. She endeavour'd, however, to shake it off; and said to Mrs. *Freelove*, I am not very well, Madam, and beg the Favour of you to excuse my coming down, 'till Supper.— No, no, replied the good Lady, If you are not well, my Dear, you shall have something sent up to you, and *Hawley*, (so her Woman was called) shall stay with you. *Emily*, glad to have an Opportunity to retire, thank'd her Benefactress for this Indulgence, and wishing both her and Sir *George* a Good-night, immediately quitted the Room.—She wou'd indeed have excused Mrs. *Hawley*'s Attendance, but that Gentlewoman paid too much Regard to her Lady's Orders, to neglect her Favourite. After a great deal of insignificant Tittle-tattle, she quitted the Room, as *Emily* pretended to be sleepy, tho' in Truth, she only wanted to get rid of a trifling Babbler.

When

When *Emily* found herself alone, she began to reflect, seriously, on Sir *George*'s Behaviour, and her own too. She was very much shock'd to think what a Part she had acted. I am afraid, said she, that I have given Sir *George* too much Reason to believe I was affected with what he said to me. O, how happy was I before I saw this Man! Yet, why shou'd the Presence of a Man, who can never be any Thing to me, give me Concern? For whether he likes me or not, I ought not to disturb myself about him, since the Discovery he made of his Sentiments To-day, convinces me he has no honourable Regard for me, and besides, if he had, he is so much superior to me in Rank and Fortune, that I dare not think of an Union with him. —Yet there have been Women raised to Titles and to Riches by generous Lovers, still more above them, than he is above me—Yet why do I indulge such flattering Thoughts?—Were Sir *George* willing to make me his Wife, could I consent to injure him in the Opinion of the World, and repay in such a Manner the maternal Kindness of Mrs. *Freelove*? No, I will think no more of him——I'll try to forget him——I soon refused the Earl, and why should I not be as ready to renounce Sir *George?* There is no Rank in Life, to which, Heaven's my Witness, I would not raise Sir *George,* were I in his Situation, and he in mine—But his Pride will not suffer him to think in so disinterested a Manner. Is such a Man then worthy of a Woman's Love? No certainly.—— Yet, what a Pity it is that a Man, who has so many engaging Accomplishments, should be a Stranger to one, which added to the Rest, would make him compleatly amiable, that is, a virtuous Disposition—As he wants *this Disposition,* he should appear despicable in my Eyes. How ridiculous was my Behaviour to him? How I long to see him again, that I may rectify my Error, and let him know that I can hate Vice in the Form of an Angel.

In this Way did *Emily* reason with herself, unable to taste the Sweets of Sleep. All Night she tossed about, and rose from her Bed in the Morning unrefreshed. Nor was Sir *George*'s Mind more at Ease. He loved her too well not to be concerned at her Indisposition, though he loved not well enough to think

think on Marriage without Aversion. Had it not been for this rooted Aversion, he might have made the most deserving Woman in the World happy, superlatively happy, for he was accountable to Nobody for his Actions, his Estate was unencumbered, and he had no *Relation* to disapprove of his Choice, but Mrs *Freelove*, from whom he had no great Expectations, as she was so firmly attached to her own Family. But he had made a Resolution never to marry, a Resolution which he did not seem capable of changing. Especially when he believed that *Emily*'s Disorder was entirely on his Account, because he conceived Hopes of being able to cure her in his own Way.

When Mrs *Hawly*, in the Morning, first came to enquire after *Emily*'s Health, she told her she was perfectly recovered, and waited directly on Mrs. *Freelove*, with the same Speech. Mrs *Freelove* expressed a great deal of Satisfaction at finding her so much better than she expected, but desired she would take the utmost Care of herself, and advised her not to eat much Fruit, to which the good Lady attributed her Disorder, little
dreaming

dreaming of the real Cause of it. *Emily* thanked her for interesting herself so much in her Behalf, and went down to Breakfast with her. Sir *George* was in the Parlour ready to receive his Aunt and his Mistress; and after bidding the former good Morrow, inquired tenderly how the latter found herself, and whether she had rested well? *Emily*, though she was not thoroughly composed at the Sight of Sir *George*, kept her Resolution, and only told him cooly, that she had slept the whole Night, and was perfectly recovered. He was not a little disconcerted at her Indifference, and could not help shewing that he was so. For though he had all the Reason in the World to believe that her Indifference was assumed, he felt an Uneasiness he could not conceal. His Aunt, as well as *Emil.*, perceived it, and asked him why he was so uncommonly thoughtful? He told her he felt a violent Pain in his Head, which had hindered him from closing his Eyes all Night. When he had made this evasive Answer to his Aunt's home Question, he watched *Emily*'s Looks, in order to find out how she received the News of his Indisposition: But she kept her Muscles so nicely disci-

disciplined, that he could not trace the least Alteration in them, either for or against him. To heighten his Suspence, she retired to her own Apartment, as soon as Mrs. *Freelove* went to pay a Visit to Mrs. *Parker* (instead of staying with him as she used to do, in the Parlour on such an Occasion) and they met not again till Dinner.

Sir *George* had, from the first Sight of *Emily*, been very studious to please her, but now he was particularly assiduous, and endeavoured to give her fresh Instances every Day of his excessive Regard for her. She received all those Instances with Respect and Civility, but grew more reserved and unfamiliar in her Behaviour to him.

Mrs. *Freelove* retired in the Afternoon, according to Custom, for about an Hour, to her Dressing-room; when she arose to go, *Emily* rose also, in order to follow her. Sir *George*, who wanted another private Interview, said to his Aunt, I wish, Madam, you would desire Miss *Willis* to stay and divert me in your Absence, for I am quite *a-la-mort* To-day, and can't bear to be alone. As

he

he spoke these Words in a jocose Way, Mrs *Freelove* answered him with as much Jocoseness, and ordered *Emily* to revive his Spirits, by playing merry Tunes, or reading a diverting Story to him, till she came down again. Poor *Emily* did not know what Excuse to make. Indeed she did not really *wish to make one*, but as a Compliance with Mrs *Freelove*'s Commands would have prevented her from pursuing the Resolutions she had formed in the Morning, she was determined to frame an Excuse. Before Sir *George* could get Time to speak, she made him a low Curtsy, and told him she was going up stairs for a music Book. Sir *George*, with a Smile of Satisfaction, bowed an Assent to her leaving the Room, not doubting, in the least, but she would instantly return. But as soon as she was safely rested in her own Apartment, she dispatched a Servant to inform him, that she was not very well, and hoped he would be so obliging as to excuse her waiting upon him at that Time.

By this Finesse *Emily* gained her Point Sir *George* being heartily vexed at her Behaviour, began to think that if he coun-

counterfeited Illness and Melancholy, he might thereby rouze her Pity and Concern, which would in all Probability, make a Change in her Conduct towards him.

They met again at Supper. Mrs *Freelove* then told them, that she believed they had agreed to be sick together, for no other Reason but to be bad Company to *her* and to each other. *Emily* assured her she was quite well again, but Sir *George* fetched a deep Sigh, and said, he was afraid he never *should* be well again.

A Week passed in this Manner, during which, Sir *George* could never meet with *Emily* alone. She all the Time endeavoured to be as chearful as she used to be, though her Mind was far from being in a peaceful State; but *he* grew worse and worse. Mrs *Freelove* was alarmed at the Increase of her Nephew's Indisposition, and could not be easy without sending for a Physician. The Family Doctor, who resided within a few Miles of *Fairly-Manor*, was, luckily for Sir *George*, a very facetious Companion, and not at all averse to a pretty
Girl.

Girl Sir *George*, therefore, easily persuaded him that a slight Regimen was absolutely necessary for a Man in his Circumstances, without telling him directly *why* such a Regimen was necessary. The Doctor, being well acquainted with his Patient's Temper and Inclinations, took care to make a palatable Prescription; but never guessed at his real Malady, as he had not had many Opportunities of seeing the Authoress of it, though he came frequently to the House.

Several Days glided away before Sir *George* found any favourable Alteration in *Emily*'s Behaviour (for she had not shewed the least Concern for him, tho' she was inwardly uneasy about him) An Accident then happened which raised his drooping Spirits, and made him ample Amends for the Anxieties he had been tortured with on her Account.

Emily set out one Morning, in order to spend the day with some young Ladies, intimately acquainted with Mrs. *Freelove*, who lived about two Miles from the Manor. Sir *George* saw her get into his Aunt's Coach with the highest
Satis-

Satisfaction, becaufe he was full of Hopes that his new Scheme to have her to himfelf, would not be defeated. He followed the Coach, on its return home in the Evening, till it was driven out of Sight of the Houfe, and then ordered the Coachman to quit his Box and open the Door. *Emily* was both furprifed and chagrined to be thus entrapped, but had very little Time to indulge either the Paffions of Aftonifhment or Vexation, for Sir *George*, attempting to get haftily into the Coach, miffed his Step and fell down. As the Horfes immediately ftarted in a mettlefome Manner, *Emily* was very much afraid that he was under the Wheels, and in the greateft Danger of being crufhed to Death. Thefe Apprehenfions foon got the better of all her affected Indifference. She fcreamed and fainted. Sir *George*, who had really received no Hurt, prefently recovered himfelf, jumped into the Coach, and ordered the Man to drive on. When he turned towards *Emily*, he was amazed to fee her in fo unhappy a Condition, and could not attribute her fainting Fit to any Thing but his too abrupt Appearance. He tried every Method he could

could think of to recal her Senses, and soon succeeded, and soon too perceived that her Fright was occasioned by his imagined Danger. This Discovery gave him great Pleasure, and made him eager to find out her real Sentiments with regard to him. He pressed her in his Arms, and thus soothingly essayed to *heal her unquiet Mind, and tune her Soul to Peace*—Be not alarmed, dear Miss *Willis*, for I shall do very well. The Hurt I have received is slight, and would give me no Disturbance if you were easy. *Emily*, who at first actually thought he had been killed, rejoiced to hear him speak so chearfully, and could not help crying out, O, Sir *George*, how excessively I have been frightened! But where are you wounded? For Heaven's Sake let *John* run for a Surgeon, as the least Delay may be attended with fatal Consequences.--Be composed, my Angel, replied Sir *George*, kissing her Cheek, which he had pressed to his Bosom, I shall not want any Assistance till we get home. How happy am I to find that I am not quite so indifferent to you as I feared I was! O could you but know how much your Coldness has distressed me, I am sure your gentle Heart would

would pity me. Life grew burdensome to me, when you treated me with Unkindness, but I am now so blest with the Marks you have shewed me of your Esteem, that I could bear the Stroke of Death without repining.—O do not talk of Death, said *Emily*, (quite overcome by Tenderness and Sorrow, which disabled her from keeping the Resolution she had made, never to reveal her Passion to him) I cannot bear to think of your dying. Let me stop the Coach and send *John* for Help this Moment — No, my dearest Creature, said he, there is no Occasion. I only beg you would listen patiently to me.—But why, said she, why do you pretend to love me, and yet neglect your own Safety, which is dearer to me than my Life?—Make yourself easy, my Love, my dearest *Emily*, replied Sir *George*, (transported with Joy that his Scheme had met with Success) I am not hurt at all. Indeed I am not. Won't you believe me when I give you so many repeated Assurances of my Welfare? I am perfectly well, my Angel, and the happiest of Men, since I have at length made the most charming of Women sensible of the Sincerity of my Passion. He accompanied

panied this Speech with several tender Caresses, which waked *Emily* from the Lethargy she had been plunged in while he uttered it, and made her see, tho' too late, her Error. She was both vexed and ashamed, yet resolved to do her utmost to repair her Fault. She withdrew from his Arms, and, blushing, said, Have you really received no Hurt, Sir?—None, my Life, said he, again seizing her Hand, but what you can cure whenever you please. He then put her Hand to his Lips in an Extacy, and thus went on. How infinitely am I obliged to my sweetest *Emily*, for interesting herself so much in my Behalf, and discovering a Secret, which I am apt to believe, she did not intend so hastily to divulge! *Emily* now began to look serious, and disengaging herself from his Clasp, replied, You are very much mistaken, Sir, if you imagine that your Design has succeeded, I see thro' all your Arts, and hope I shall have Prudence enough to baffle them. I own I was frightened, when I thought you were dangerously hurt, but I should also have been so to have seen a Stranger in the same Situation: Though perhaps, added she, with glowing Cheeks, not

not so much concerned as I was for you. But the Trap you have laid for me, I cannot approve of. You have, by acting so clandestinely, cured me of all my Prejudices in your Favour, and I now look on you with more than Indifference, I look on you with Aversion. I look on you as my greatest Enemy, and as the avowed Destroyer of my present and my future Peace.

Good Heavens, Madam, cried Sir *George*, how grossly are you deceived! Can the truest Professions of the tenderest Friendship for you make me appear to you in so odious, so detestable a Light?—I have no great Opinion, Sir *George*, said *Emily*, of such a Friendship, and shall always treat the Man who solicits me to be his Mistress, as I would my declared and most virulent Enemy.——Is it impossible then, Miss *Willis*, replied Sir *George*, for me to convince you that there is no pure Happiness in this World without *mutual* Love, and that *Love* hardly ever subsists but in an Union which is prompted by Inclination and unfettered by Duty?—It will always be impossible, said she, to convince me that we can be happy

without

without being virtuous. — I should be glad, Madam, said he, to hear your Definition of Virtue. For my Part, I am inclined to think that two Persons are very virtuous, if they endeavour to promote each other's Happiness, without injuring their Fellow-creatures. Can a Woman of Miss *Willis*'s Sagacity be so bigotted to Custom, as to imagine that she is not strictly virtuous while she loves one Man fondly, and is attached solely to him? Or can she think that she would be more virtuous, because a Priest muttered a few insignificant Words over her?—I have always, Sir *George*, said *Emily*, avoided an Argument on this Subject with *you*, or indeed any of your Sex, but since you force me into it, I shall answer you in your own Way, that is, by Interrogatories. Pray, Sir, if you had a Sister in my Situation, would you chuse to have her united to a Man in an illegal Manner? Sir *George* was somewhat posed by this home Question, but soon replied with his usual Vivacity. — The Custom of the World, said he, might perhaps induce me to blame her Conduct, in Public, though I should not in my Heart severely condemn it. But what

what have you and I to do with Custom, Miss *Willis?* continued he, I am entirely at Liberty, and you need not fear, or care for any Thing when you are under my Protection —And can a Desire to lessen me in the Opinion of the World, said *Emily,* be a Proof of true Regard? No, Sir, you can have no Esteem for a Woman whom you would render contemptible, and without Esteem, Love can be but a short-lived-Passion. Nay, you would yourself despise a fond Creature, after you had made her despicable in the Eye of the World ——Why despise her? said Sir *George.* But you don't know me. Your Compliance with my Requests would endear you so much to me, that I should love you for ever. And if I loved you, you ought to be as indifferent about a censorious World, as if you were actually married —— But the World, said *Emily,* would not be indifferent about *me* — Then I find, said he, that Custom is the only Bar to my Happiness, and that you don't think my Scheme wrong yourself, but are afraid that others will condemn it Indeed, Miss *Willis,* you ought to be above these little foolish Prejudices.

You are endued with numberless Beauties, both personal and intellectual, but you are endued with them to no Purpose, if you intend not to make use of them. Come, my Angel, continued he, once more seizing her Hand, you was not made to be a Slave to that tyrant Custom. Be assured, that making the Man who dies for you, happy, you will stand the fairest Chance to be happy yourself.—You and I, Sir *George,* said *Emily,* with more Haughtiness than she had ever assumed, are of a different Opinion on this Subject. I am neither to be lulled by Flattery, nor out-witted by Sophistry. I am determined to be Virtuous in the strictest Acceptation of the Word, and therefore shall take it as a Favour if you would never talk to me again on this Subject. As they were now very near their Journey's End, Sir *George* dropp'd the Conversation, and only signified his Obedience, by a Motion of his Head and a deep Sigh.

As soon as they enter'd the House, Sir *George* told his Aunt, that he expected to have found her in her Equipage, when he met it, and that he was not a little chagrin'd at his Disappointment.

This

This Compliment wou'd, he imagined, pleafe the old Lady, and prevent her making any Reflections that might be difagreeable to him on his coming Home with *Emily.* But tho' his *Aunt* was fo eafily blinded, all the Servants were quick-fighted enough, and plainly perceiv'd that Sir *George* was very fond of Mifs *Willis*'s Company.

It was with great Difficulty that *Emily* conceal'd the Emotion, which her laft Interview with Sir *George* had occafion'd. But fhe difguis'd her Uneafinefs as well as fhe cou'd, and carefully fhunn'd him, except at thofe Times when fhe knew they fhou'd not be left alone. She often retired to her Chamber, to give Vent to her Sorrows, and often, in her Moments of Privacy, blamed herfelf, for loving a Man fo unworthy of a Woman's Efteem. And never reflected on the Difcovery fhe had made of her Regard for him, without being filled with Shame and Vexation.

As for Sir *George*, he had ftill Hopes, from the natural Tendernefs of her Difpofition, that he fhou'd conquer all her Refolutions againft him, as the Coach

Adventure had convinced him, that he had some Command over her Affections. He continued to feign Illness, and strove, by every Art he was Master of, to excite her Compassion, well-knowing that Compassion and Love are very nearly allied.

At the End of a Fortnight, Sir *George* grew weary of acting the Part of a sick Man, finding it to be of no Service to him, and really became melancholy, receiving no Consolation but from the Recollection of those happy Moments which he enjoy'd in the Coach, when the charming *Emily* sunk in his Arms, and gave a loose to the Dictates of her Heart.

About this Time a young Man of Quality, one of Sir *George*'s particular Companions, (who was going to pay a Visit to his Father) called at the *Manor*, on hearing his Friend was there, in order to spend a Day with him.

Lord *William Fashion* had a very tolerable Person, a good Understanding, and a polite Address. With these Accomplishments he passed for a pretty Gentleman,

man, among the decent People of both Sexes. But when he was not over-awed by the Presence of such People, he discovered a Set of the loosest Principles. He took particular Notice of *Emily*, while they were at Dinner, and when Mrs. *Freelove* and *she* retired, after the Cloth was removed, thus open'd his Mind to his Friend.—That's a devilish fine Girl, Sir *George*, where did thy Aunt pick her up? She seems to be brought here on Purpose for thy Use. Egad thou art a lucky Dog, to have such a luscious Morsel drop into thy Mouth thus!—Indeed, my Friend, replied Sir *George*, you are out in your Reckoning: I have no more Share in her than you have.—Then, said Lord *William*, you have mispent your Time most confoundedly, or must be as blind as a Beetle to the Charms of a young, plump, juicy, sprightly Girl.—Out again, replied Sir *George*, I am not so frozen as you seem to think me, but this dear, adorable, bewitching Girl is not easily to be come at.—Not to be come at? said Lord *William*, then I am damnably mistaken indeed. Why she has the true roguish Twinkle in her Eye, and looks as if she could be very civil to

a brisk,

a brisk, well-built young Fellow.—She is certainly the most delightful Creature, said Sir *George*, I ever met with, and if you had but convers'd with her alone, as much as I have, you wou'd be as ready to run mad for her as I am.—Faith *George*, said Lord *William*, you deal in Riddles To-day. prythee speak to be understood, for I can't for my Soul guess at your Meaning. Have you been alone, say you, with such a divine Girl, and yet pretend you have had nothing to do with her? But I suppose you think I have a Design upon her myself, and perhaps I might, if she was at Liberty, but if you have struck the first Blow, I give you Joy with all my Heart. I am a Man of too much Honour to trip up my Friend's Heels in an Affair with a fine Woman!—Pshaw, pshaw, said Sir *George*, I tell you I can't make any Thing of her, and am half distracted at my Disappointment.—Not make any Thing of her? said Lord *William*; Zounds Man, then you have not begun your Attack like an experienced Officer. Here must have been some cursed Mismanagement, some blundering Doings, I see, for the Girl seems to be of a mighty gentle, loving Nature.—She is indeed, said

said Sir *George*, of a gentle loving Nature. O *Fashion*, did you but know how much Anxiety I have endured on this dear Creature's Account, you wou'd not let fly so much Raillery at me. He then, at his Lordship's Request, gave an exact Detail of *Emily*'s Behaviour and his own, from his first Arrival at *Holly-Moor*, and concluded his Narrative by protesting he loved her most extravagantly, and cou'd never be happy without her — Well, well, said Lord *William*, I'll lay you what you will that she is your own in less than a Fortnight, if you play your Cards with Judgment — Aye, but how, how, my Lord, said Sir *George*, which Way? for you see I have tried several Schemes to no Purpose — Upon my Soul, replied Lord *William*, I never saw a poor Fellow so soon disconcerted. Why you used to be a Man of Fire, but this pretty, little, skittish Toad has made you so extremely meek, that you have not Courage enough to talk Bawdy to a *Bunter*, yet this pretty little Toad loves you—Do you really think so, said Sir *George*? I was once of that Opinion, and acted accordingly. —And what cou'd induce you, said Lord *William*, to alter your

Con-

Conduct? She loves you fondly, I am sure she does, and has only a few Scruples arising from the virtuous Education your pious Aunt has given her, I suppose. Damn these old Women, can't they be quiet when they are past the Sport themselves, without preaching to the young Ones, and bidding them not make use of their Teeth, because they can only mumble?—No Invectives against my Aunt, I beseech you, my Lord, said Sir *George*; she is a good Woman, and kind to my *Emily*, and I shall not be able to hear her lightly spoken of without Resentment. If you can tell me of any Method to gain the Affections of this coy, but amiable Creature, I'll thank you from my Soul. —Her *Affections?* said Lord *William*, her Person you mean; and, if I was in your Place, I wou'd be Master of *that* in a few Hours.—How, how, dear *Fashion?* said Sir *George,* eagerly — Why, there are two Ways, replied his Lordship; but as you are in a violent Hurry, you will undoubtedly chuse the quickest. She lies alone, doesn't she?—Faith I can't tell, said Sir *George,* but I believe she does.— Well then, said my Lord, you have nothing to do but to infuse a

proper

proper Quantity of Laudanum into whatever Liquor she takes last at Night, which may be done without giving the least Room for Suspicion. That Infusion will throw her into a sound Sleep, and then you may securely feast on her Beauties, and conquer her with the greatest Ease —Sir *George*, fond as he was of a pretty Bedfellow, started at this hellish Proposal, and was just going to express his Abhorrence of it, when my Lord thus interrupted him.— If you don't care to venture on this Scheme in your Aunt's House, continued he, with a Sneer, for whom you have I see some Respect, because I suppose you expect a handsome Sum at her Death, tho' 'tis ten to one but she leaves all her Fortune to her old waiting Gentlewoman, or to the Foundling-Hospital But if you don't care, I say, to venture on the Scheme at Home, why rave lustily against the Girl before your Aunt, trump up some Story to make her Character suspected, and get her turn'd out of Doors. And when she is quite friendless, and pennyless, her Pride will be lower'd, and she will become the most compliant Creature breathing And then,

then, you or I, or the Devil may have her for a Trifle.

Sir *George* stood amazed for a considerable Time, at the villanous Schemes which Lord *Fashion* had proposed with a careless, jocular Air, but at last his Indignation prompted him to say, in a raised and resolute Tone, And do you really, my Lord, give me this diabolical Advice? Can the Man that calls himself my Friend, persuade me to be deaf to the Cries of injured Innocence, or to take Advantage of Beauty and Virtue in Distress? No, Lord *William*, I am not the Libertine you take me to be, nor am I so lost to Honour, as you falsely imagine, but suppose I were thus abandon'd, my Inclination for the lovely, injured Girl (for injured she is by your loose Opinion of her) is not of so criminal a Kind I cannot enjoy any Woman by Force, nor take Pleasure in possessing the finest *Person* in the World, without the Heart. You are not well acquainted with my Character. I love *Emily*, 'tis true, and long, impatiently long, to be possessed of all her Beauties; but I long to possess them with her own Consent I would have her fondly re-
sign

sign all her Charms to me, and share my Raptures.—Why so she wou'd, cried my Lord after the first Half-hour, take my Word for it, but I suppose the cunning Gipsy only makes you keep your Distance, in order to make your amorous Appetite the more keen. Or, perhaps, continued he, sneeringly, she may have a Fancy to be Lady *Belove*. Faith, 'tis not unlikely but she may succeed, as you are so scrupulous. Hey, Sir *George*, perhaps you will, in a Fit of the Qualms, take the Girl *for better and for worse*.—No, Sir, replied Sir *George*, gravely, I shall not marry her, I wou'd chuse to merit, and obtain her Affection, by the sincerest Tenderness, but I hate Marriage. I wou'd win her Love, and be true to her, as I believe she (cou'd I prevail on her to consent to my Plan) wou'd to me. I have the highest Opinion of her good Sense and Virtue, and will not bear to hear her defamed. As to the Scruples you are pleased to be so merry about, I am not ashamed of them. Every honest Man ought, I think, to have the same. I detest and abhor the Means you have proposed. They are superlatively brutal, and must appear shocking to those who have not

quite

quite divested themselves of Humanity. I shall always *scruple*, added he, with a particular Earnestness, to be a Villain.

Lord *William* did not much relish his Friend's last Speech, as it seemed to be introductory to a Quarrel, which he never had any Intention to provoke: He therefore replied, coolly, O Sir, 'tis mighty well; pray act as you think proper. You asked my Opinion of the Girl, and I gave it you in Jest; but if you are disposed to be serious about her, I will call on you another Day, when I happen to be in the same Humour. Here, *Tom*, continued he, addressing himself to his Servant, bring my Horse directly. He then snatch'd up his Hat, and rode away without taking Leave of any Body. Sir *George* was glad to get rid of him, and therefore made no Effort to detain him. *Emily* too was highly pleased at his Departure, for she had overheard all the Altercation about herself, and dreaded an open Rupture, both on her own and Sir *George*'s Account. But though Lord *William*'s Retreat had quieted her Fears, it could not restore her Tranquility. She had heard

heard too many of Sir *George*'s Sentiments to be unagitated: She was charmed with him for having such a good Opinion of her, and for shewing so much Disapprobation of his Companion's infamous Proposals; but she could not help sighing, when she reflected on the Aversion he discovered to Marriage. How near, said she, would this Man be to Perfection, could he but conquer this Foible! But suppose he could get the better of his Aversion to Marriage, he must not think of me, nor I of him, for if he should endeavour to make me his Wife, the World, as well as Lord *Fashion*, would say I had drawn him in. How nobly he vindicated me from the Aspersions cast on me by his dissolute Companion! I ought to esteem him for that Vindication, but I must go no farther. And let me always remember, that the more amiable he is, the more Reason have I to be upon my Guard. He must be avoided; for an Intimacy with so insinuating a Man, may be attended with very unhappy Consequences.

In a few Days after Lord *Fashion*'s Departure, Lady *Caroline* returned to *Fairly-Manor*. She had left her *Aunt* abruptly,

abruptly, in order to receive the Addresses of a Man of Quality, who had made Application to the Earl, her Father, but soon met with a heavy Disappointment, for her Right Honourable Lover, after a few Interviews with her, withdrew his Addresses, because her Father insisted on a Settlement which he thought too large. This Disappointment mortified Lady *Caroline* exceedingly, (because Lord *Shirley* was very agreeable, and had an immense Estate) and made no great Addition to her natural Sweetness of Temper. She arrived at *Fairly-Manor*, however, in tolerable Spirits, as Sir *George Freelove* was there. But her Spirits began to flag soon after her Arrival, for she perceived, in a Day or two, that he entirely neglected her. She was, at first, at a Loss to assign a Reason for the Coldness of his Behaviour, (though she had a good deal of Penetration) not having the least Notion of his being able to cast a Look on so low a Creature as *Emily*, when a Woman of her Beauty and Quality was present. But Mrs *Prate*, her Ladyship's Confidante, in a little while undeceived her, and rouzed

her

her Resentment against her innocent Rival.

One Morning Lady *Caroline*, after her Return from a Walk in the Park with Sir *George* and *Emly*, (in which she had received fresh Proofs of his Indifference) in order to dress before Dinner, she threw herself in a fretful Air upon her Settee in her Chamber, and was thus harangued by the talkative Mis *Prate*. Your La'ship seems uncommonly fatigued To-day. I hope your La'ship's not ill?—Fatigued? said my Lady, aye, 'tis enough to kill one to walk at that monstrous Rate. I sat down twenty Times, but Sir *George* was always starting up again —La, Ma'am, what does your La'ship think? said *Prate*, all the Servants says that Sir *George* is fallen in Love with Miss *Willis*—Will your La'ship wear your shot Lustring Night-gown To-day, or your Pink Negligee?--Pr'ythee, *Prate*, replied Lady *Caroline*, don't ask so many impertinent Questions Sir *George* in Love with that Creature, do you say? It cannot be Where are his Eyes?—Aye, said *Prate*, where indeed, my Lady? I think I can see as well as other Folks, and to
be

be sure I can't find any Beauty in her, though all the Fellows below says she is the prettiest Girl they ever beheld in all their Lives.—They are fine Judges of Beauty indeed, said Lady *Caroline*, how should they know the Difference between Handsomeness and Ugliness? But Sir *George* surely must have a Taste. He, who converses with all the fine Women in Town, cannot, I am persuaded, allow such a hoydening Chit to be tolerable. In the first Place, she is vastly coarse; then she has always such a violent Colour—— Yes, indeed, said *Prate*, so she has, my Lady, and it is always worst when Sir *George* is in the Room, if your La'ship minds.— Aye, aye, said Lady *Caroline*, I suppose the conceited Thing is in Love with him, and is afraid of being found out by me and my Aunt. I know Sir *George*, I think, better than to imagine he would trouble his Head about such an insignificant Wretch.— I don't know, indeed, said *Prate*, but Sir *George*'s Valet, my Lady, says that his Master is the most altered he ever knew a Man in all his born Days, since Miss *Willis* came to *Fairly-Manor*.—Miss *Willis*! replied Lady *Caroline*, a pretty *Miss* truly! *Emily* is her Name, and she deserves no Addition to it.— Nay to be sure your La'ship's in the right, said *Prate*, she has no more Business to be called *Miss* than I have; for she only waits on Mrs. *Freelove*, as I do on your La'ship. Not but that I was called Miss *Fanny* in my last Place, Lady *Overall*'s, because she could not bear any Sound in her Family that was mean and vulgar. And to tell your La'ship the Truth, I think myself every bit and crum as good as Miss *Willis*, for all she is so pretty.—— *Miss* again! cried Lady *Caroline*, in a Pet, I won't have you grate my Ears with your odious, ill-placed Appellations. I tell you the Thing is *not* pretty. A poor lifeless Ideot —— pretty indeed!—— Nay I am sure, said *Prate*, I am glad to have your La'ship of my Ideas, for I always said from the Beginning, when they cried up her clear Complexion, bright Eyes, and easy Shape, that she was just for all the World like a great Doll; tall and awkward, with two large Cherry Cheeks, and a Couple of black Sawcer Eyes.— Well, said Lady *Caroline*, laughing heartily, I declare, *Prate*, you have drawn her to the Life: Her Complexion

might

might be well enough if it wasn't always mudled with Scarlet, and her Eyes 'tis true are large, but they are likewise the most unmeaning Gogglers I ever beheld. She doesn't know how to make Use of them. Then I don't believe she is quite strait, for sure 'tis the stiffest Creature!——No Air——No Mien—But how should Girls, raised from an obscure Station, be genteel? Nor indeed is it fit they should. People who are born to be Servants should not attempt to vie with their Betters. But I can't imagine, *Prate,* how you came to fancy that Sir *George* likes such an awkward Soul. He is civil to her, I suppose, out of Respect to his Aunt, who, by the bye, pays both of us but a poor Compliment, in bringing such mean Wretches amongst us.—— To be sure, my Lady, replied *Prate*, the Girl has bewitched Madam *Freelove,* otherwise she wou'd never be so fond of her. Mrs *Hawley* says that never any thing was like it. And Mrs. *Hawley* hates her as she hates the Devil, because she is afraid she will put her out of Favour with her Mistress. Now, to be sure, it will be vastly ungenerous in Mrs. *Freelove*, to turn off an old faithful Servant

vant to make room for an awkward, pert young Hussey — Well, well, said Lady *Caroline*, don't fatigue me with Mrs. *Hawley*, and her Fears, and her Fancies, I want to know what Reason you have for believing that Sir *George* likes her, though I am sure he does not — Why, indeed my Lady, said *Prate*, Mr *Frifeur* says, that he is certain Sir *George* is over Head and Ears in Love with her, and believes that a Marriage will —— A Marriage! cried Lady *Caroline*, in a violent Heat, Heaven forbid! He cannot dream of that I hope, nor will the infolent Wretch dare, I believe, to attempt fuch a thing But left fhe fhould, I'll endeavour to root her out of the Family. I'll go directly to my Aunt, and tell her all I know about this Affair.

Oh, dear my Lady, faid *Prate*, (who began to be frightened) let me beg you not to mention a Syllable of what I have been faying to your La'fhip, for poor Mr. *Frifeur* will lofe his Place, perhaps, and that would be a thoufand Pities, for he is the civilleft beft tempered—— Hold your Nonfenfe, *Prate*, faid Lady *Caroline*, what's his Civility
to

to me? I suppose, if the Truth were known, you intend to draw him in for a Husband, as you are so sanguine in his Behalf — *I* draw him in? No, indeed, my Lady, said *Prate*, perking up her Head, I would have your Ladyship to know, that I scorn such wicked Doings. Besides, I hope, I am above a *French Valee de Chambre*. I that have refused so many good Gentlemen's Offers. There was Mr *Cash*, Sir *Francis*'s Steward, and Mr. *Corkum* the Butler — For Heaven's Sake, cried Lady *Caroline*, stop that eternal Clack of yours, and don't think of entertaining me with your dirty Amours. — Dirty? my Lady, Dirty? said *Prate*. — Hold your Tongue, replied her Ladyship very sternly, when I bid you, I will not be worried at this rate. Get my Things to Dress, I'll go this Minute to my Aunt. — Just as her Ladyship was going to put her Design in execution, (to the no small Mortification of Mrs. *Prate*, who endeavoured to retard her Flight, by pinning and unpinning her Handkerchief) a Servant came up to inform her that Dinner waited. — There now, said Lady *Caroline*, you tedious Bungler, what's the Reason I am not ready?

dy? But you chatter so perpetually, that you never know what you are about. Put on my Negligée this Instant—no—stay—let it alone—I'll go as I am. My Aunt shall see what a Drozzel you are.— O Lud, continued she, looking in the Glass, what a *Fright* the Wench has made me to Day! Why, you have braided my Hair no broader than your little Finger.——Here—fetch me the Powder to hide it—and you know I abominate Powder. *Prate*, who found her Lady was very much displeased, either with her, or her News, and was moreover afraid lest Mr *Friseur* should be dismissed, (whose Addresses she received, after the Example of much finer Ladies than herself, at the very Time she affected to despise them) began to have recourse to a Remedy which may justly be called an universal one, because it never fails of Success—— Flattery. She was also the more inclined to make Use of that same Remedy, as it generally had a very wonderful Effect on the Constitution of her Lady.—I wonder, Ma'am, said *Prate*, that your La'ship will find such Fault with yourself to Day, and be so angry with me, when I vow I never saw you look

look so charmingly in all my Life. To be sure, I am always very sorry to have your La'ship's Displeasure, but upon my Word, your La'ship looks most enchanting whenever your La'ship is a little ruffled at any Thing, it gives such a Spirit to your Eyes, and Bloom to your Complexion.—So, so, *Prate*, said my Lady, smiling, I shall fancy I have a Lover with me if you run on thus— but do I really look tolerably?— Yes, my Lady, cried *Prate*, delightfully I am most sure. *Emily* is not to be named the same Day, with your La'ship.— *Emily!* replied her Ladyship disdainfully, I hope I have not the most distant Resemblance of that saudling Mawkin. She is quite a Doll indeed, as you said, *Prate*, but you do say just Things enough sometimes. There—you may take these blond Ruffles, I shan't wear them again. Just at this Juncture, the Footman made his second Appearance, with Mrs. *Freelove*'s Compliments, who wanted to know if her Ladyship chose to go down to Dinner, or to have a *Plate* in her Dressing-room. The Devil's in the Dinner, said Lady *Caroline*, and my Aunt too, I think, with her formal Message.—Tell her I am coming,

ing, said she to the Servant—Stay, continued she to *Prate*, I won't go till I have a Patch on this Place, just by my left Eye—Let me see the Box—take away your fiddling Fingers, you have a Mind to blind me, I verily believe—Deuce take the Wench, had it not been for you, I should have been ready an Hour ago—Why did you not dress me?—I only waited for your La'ship's Orders, said *Prate*—Waited for a Fiddle-stick, said Lady *Caroline*, you knew well enough I was to be dressed, and have not I told you a thousand Times to dress me whether I will or no?—La, said *Prate*, I'm sure I durst not touch your La'ship, without your La'ship's Orders—You are a Fool, said Lady *Caroline* Now had I as lieve go to the Devil as to dine with my Aunt *Freelove*, for I know she will snub me before Sir *George*, and positively I will not bear it. When she had finished this Sentence, she was just got to the Top of the Stairs, but ran hastily back to her Glass, and cried, Here, *Prate*, give me the *Rouge*, for I have fretted myself into a Paleness to Day, and if I come near that Girl, I shall look as white as a Napkin, for she has naturally such an odious Complexion, and Colours so excessively when any Body speaks to her—Now that Colouring is a certain Sign with me of low Breeding. Did you ever see a Woman of Birth or Fashion Blush? No, they know better. There is nothing in Life so ridiculous as what is commonly called Modesty. Every Woman who knows the World is above it.——To be sure, my Lady, said *Prate*, it looks vastly silly to be always out of Countenance.—Silly! said her Ladyship, 'tis ten thousand Times worse, for I never see a Woman blush, but I conclude she has been doing what she should not. I am sure, *Prate*, you must be mistaken about Sir *George*. He never can think of her.—Lack-a-day, my Lady, said *Prate*, (who found she might make something of her Informations) why should not Sir *George* like her, as well as my Lord? Fancy passes Beauty, and I suppose your La'ship would rather call her Cousin, than Sister.——Sister! cried Lady *Caroline*, O Heavens! what does the Wench mean? Why my Brother has not been much here since my Aunt took this little Minx into her House. He can know nothing of her.—I can't say, indeed, my my Lady, what his Lordship knows, said *Prate*, or what he doesn't know, but I am pretty well assured he has offered her Marriage ———O, I shall die at the Thought of it, replied Lady *Caroline*, I'll go this Moment to my Aunt, and get her turned out of the House. A saucy Flirt, to pretend to *my* Brother!———Pray, good your La'ship, cried *Prate*, don't mention my Name to Madam *Freelove*. When your La'ship has dined, I can tell you a great deal more.—Do, do, dear *Prate*, said Lady *Caroline*, eagerly, I will pretend to be out of Humour with my Aunt after Dinner, for I know she will give me Cause, and come up into my Dressing-room. She then bounced down to the Parlour, and took the Seat left for her at Mrs *Freelove*'s Right-hand, who told her they had almost dined, and rebuked her gently for making them stay so long for her in this Manner. For the Future, Lady *Caroline*, I beg you would stay in your own Apartment, when you are out of Humour, or not dressed. I do not chuse to have my Family Hours broke in upon. Lady *Caroline* reddened with Anger at this Reprimand, but, without making any

Reply, began to amuse herself with the Rump of a Chicken. While she was so employed, Sir *George*, who always took particular Notice of *Emily*, observed that her Plate was empty, and desired her to help herself to a Wing of one of the Partridges which stood at her Elbow. This Request heightened the Colouring in Lady *Caroline*'s Cheeks, and extorted the following Answer. I believe, Sir, these Birds were drest on purpose for my Aunt, and I hope *Emily* is not so nice but that she can find something else to eat: She was not born to digest such Dainties. This unexpected Speech, with the haughty Air which accompanied it, filled Sir *George* with the utmost Indignation. Poor *Emily*, quite shocked at the Rudeness of her Behaviour, desired, with a Blush, that she might be helped to any Thing else upon the Table. But Mrs *Freelove*, who was greatly astonished at her Niece's Freedom, smartly reprimanded her, by saying, I don't understand you to Day, Lady *Caroline*, you really seem in a very pretty Humour, but I shan't encourage it, I can assure you. I desire, Miss *Willis*, continued she, addressing herself to *Emily*, you will help yourself to a Partridge, while I inform my Niece that she has no Command at *my* Table. I am at Liberty to entertain who I think proper, and whoever offers to interpose, will very soon find that I have Resolution enough not to be directed in my own House. Take the Partridge, Child, I say, (perceiving that *Emily* modestly declined it) while you are under my Protection, I will take care that you shall not be insulted. Sir *George*, highly pleased with Mrs. *Freelove*'s spirited Speech, eagerly conveyed a Partridge to *Emily*, who received it with some Confusion, not being able to guess at the Cause of this Bustle on her Account, while Lady *Caroline* was ready to burst with Envy and Rage, and it was with the greatest Difficulty she kept her Passions within bounds. For Sir *George* behaved more respectfully to *Emily* than ever, to make her Amends for his Cousin's Rudeness, and paid her a thousand Civilities, in order to raise her Spirits, which were greatly depressed.

Mrs. *Freelove* seemed to approve of her Nephew's good-natured Behaviour to *Emily*, and, after the Cloth was removed, said to him, I have a great Mind to take a little Airing, this Afternoon, Sir *George*, will you give me and *Emily* your Company? What say you to the Scheme? Lady *Caroline*, I suppose, is otherwise engaged. Sir *George* assured his Aunt that he would attend her with the greatest Satisfaction, while Lady *Caroline*, though she longed to be left alone with *Prate*, was terribly mortified that she had not been allowed to chuse whether she would go Abroad, or stay at Home. She pouted and bit her Lips till the Coffee-things were taken away, and then flounced out of the Room.

Mrs. *Freelove*, soon after her Niece's rude Departure, retired to make some Alteration in her Dress, and left Sir *George* and *Emily* alone. Sir *George*, who had long wished for a *Tête-a-tête*, gently seized her Hand and said, How much have I been shocked to Day, Miss *Willis*, at Lady *Caroline*'s Behaviour to you! But I hope you will not let that or any Thing else give you Uneasiness, while my Aunt is so sincerely your Friend. How much more amiable are you, than that giddy, haughty, conceited

ceited Creature, and how infinitely superior indeed to all your Sex! Be not therefore surprised or offended, dear *Emily*, that I love you, (though you shun me) with the same unabated Passion. Your *Person*, blooming and engaging as it is, I look upon as the least of your Perfections. I am more charmed with the Sweetness of your Disposition, the Mildness of your Affections, your great Delicacy and Sensibility, and the Discreetness you discover (so unlike are you to the common Run of Females at your Time of Life) in all your Actions. I am particularly pleased with your Conduct towards Lord *B*———, (for I have heard that you refused his Addresses) and am thoroughly convinced that your Heart is more valuable than Gems or Gold. O could I but possess so rich a Prize!—— *Emily* blushed, sighed, withdrew her Hand and seemed in greater Confusion than ever, which Sir *George* attributed to the Discovery he had made of his Knowledge about her Affairs with Lord *B*———, and thus went on —Be not ashamed, dear Miss *Willis*, at my knowing of your Behaviour to Lord *B*———. It was communicated to me by his Lordship himself, and has raised you very high in my Esteem. I have not had an Opportunity to mention it before, nor did I think it necessary till now, and now I mention it, in order to persuade you to give yourself no Concern about the *Sister*, since the *Brother* thinks you worthy of sharing his Title and his Fortune. I own I am quite delighted with you for rejecting his Marriage Offer, because I have the Satisfaction to find, that (in the first Place) he is not agreeable to you, and that (in the second) you will not give your Hand without your Heart.—*Emily* was just going to make a Reply, which would break off a Conversation she feared would be too long, but Mrs. *Trelace* saved her the Trouble, by calling her to get into the Coach.

Emily was highly pleased both with her Airing, and her Company. Sir *George* appeared uncommonly agreeable in her Eyes; for his repeated Civilities, upon the ill Behaviour of Lady *Caroline*, and his Assurances of unabated Love, had softened her Heart, and made her throw off a great deal of her Reserve, though Mrs. *Trelace*'s Presence hindered ed her from discovering her real Sentiments in his Favour.

Lady *Caroline*, during the Absence of her Aunt and her Cousin, was closeted with *Prate*, who told her every Thing she had collected from the Servants; and she in return communicated to her *Woman* what Sir *George* had said to *Emily*, when they were left alone, (having placed herself in a private Corner in order to listen) with a few Alterations and Additions of her own, to make *Emily* appear in an odious Light. Sir *George*, said she, has accused the Girl of endeavouring to draw in Lord B——, but she shall play no more Tricks in this House. I'll do her Business for her, I warrant, as soon as my *Aunt* comes in: But I shall say nothing of Sir *George*, since what I shall say about my Brother, will be sufficient to ruin her.—To be sure, said *Prate*, (who rejoiced to hear Sir *George* was not to be mentioned, for Mr. *Frisem*'s Sake) she is not to blame here, for I verily *believe* s Sir *George* wanted to make a Madam of her, and for certain, *she* wanted to be my Lady—I'll my Lady her, said Lady *Caroline*, I'll teach her to think of *my* Brother. An insolent Huffy! I shall think every Minute an Hour till my Aunt comes in —As soon as she had spoken these Words, Mrs. *Freelove* arrived.

Lady *Caroline* accosted her Aunt with the highest good Humour, but as her Aunt had resented her former Behaviour, she only told her she was glad to find such an Alteration in her Temper, and desired to speak with her in her Dressing-Room. Lady *Caroline* had been wishing for such a Proposal, and attended her directly. Mrs. *Freelove*, after having dispatched *Emily* to her own Apartment, thus addressed her Niece. Indeed, my dear Lady *Caroline*, I never was so angry with you in my Life as I was at Dinner. You made me wait a long While for you, and when you came, you assumed too much Pride and Arrogance over poor *Emily*, who is a good mild Girl, and does not deserve such Usage. Besides, if she was not so good and so mild a Girl, she ought to be treated with Respect at my Table, as a Person whom I have thought proper to place at it. Those who treat *her* disrespectfully affront *me*, and I shall always

ways desire such **People** to leave the Room; for I *will* have who I like to dine with me.

Dear Madam, said Lady *Caroline*, with a fawning Air, I am vastly sorry that I was not ready for Dinner; but *Prate* was to blame, I assure you. She is so long a-dressing me every Day, that she almost makes me crazy. But as for *Emily*, Madam, if you knew how much you are deceived in her, you wou'd rather applaud than condemn me for my Behaviour to her. O Madam, you don't know what a sly Creature she is!—I know, replied Mrs. *Freelove*, warmly, that you, as well as the rest of the Family, are vext because I shew Favour to that poor Child, who is in a Manner friendless, and every Way deserving of my Kindness.—I vext, said Lady *Caroline*, looking as red as an incens'd Turky-Cock, I vext? No indeed, Madam, I am not jealous of such low Wretches, but I own I shou'dn't like to call her Sister, however deserving you may think her Nor wou'd you, I believe, Madam, chuse to honour her with the Name of Niece.—Niece and Sister! What do you mean, Child? said Mrs. *Freelove* hastily.

—No more than I can prove, Madam, replied Lady *Caroline* as hastily. She has long had a Design on Lord *B——*, and I am afraid will persuade him, by her insinuating Arts (for he is desperately smitten with her) to marry her—Marry her? said Mrs *Freelove*, full of Astonishment, your Brother marry *Emily?* It can't be—It *shan't* be, Madam, said Lady *Caroline*, if I can possibly prevent it. But it is certain that she is carrying on such a Scheme, tho' she has driven him from the House, as all the Servants can witness, and now she is playing her Tricks with Sir *George*, to see if she can bring my Brother to her Purpose by making him jealous of his Cousin. O she is the artfullest little Witch I ever heard of!—And have you been telling me nothing but the Truth all this While? said Mrs. *Freelove*.—Nothing but the Truth, upon my Honour, Madam, said Lady *Caroline*. I overheard Sir *George* tax her this Afternoon with it, tho' I know he will deny he did, for Fear you should suspect him of wanting to seduce the Girl; but I actually heard him talk to her about my Brother, this Afternoon: but if you won't believe me, Madam, pray call my *Woman* and

and Mrs *Hawley.* They will both of them tell you how monstrously you are imposed upon by that thorough-paced Hypocrite.—No, said Mrs *Freelove*, there's no Occasion to bring the Servants to prove what you say. I don't suppose, Lady *Caroline*, you are capable of inventing a Story, merely to blacken the Girl's Character. But you must give me Leave to examine *Emily* myself —Oh by all Means, Madam, replied Lady *Caroline*, but she will certainly deny every Tittle of it.—I don't know that, said Mrs *Freelove* (ringing her Bell) I am greatly mistaken, if *Emily* is not an honest Girl. But if I find she has deceived me in the least Thing in the World, she shall immediately quit my House. When she had finished her Speech, Mrs. *Hawley* appear'd, to know her Commands. Bid *Emily* come to me directly, said she to Mrs. *Hawley*; I must intreat *your* Absence a few Minutes, continued she to her Niece. Lady *Caroline* was very well pleas'd to be dismiss'd, and ran after Mrs *Hawley*, and desired she would come to her Room, as soon as she had sent *Emly* to her Aunt. Mrs *Hawley*, not finding *Emly* in her own Apartment, dispatch'd one of the

Maids to search further, and hurried away to know what Lady *Caroline* had to say to her. When the following Dialogue pass'd between them.

I have discovered, said Lady *Caroline*, a Plot, Mrs. *Hawley*; *Emily Willis* has Designs upon my Brother and Sir *George*. I have acquainted my Aunt with them, but she is so prepossess'd in the Girl's Favour, that I am afraid she will keep her in her Family, unless you will declare that what I have been saying, is true. I am sure what I have been saying *is* true; but my Aunt perhaps may question *you*, and 'tis better you shou'd be prepar'd you know I am ready to die, I declare, at the Thoughts of my Brother's marrying such a Girl, therefore, dear Mrs *Hawley*, let us get her out of the Family. Pray accept of this Trifle (giving her a Guinea) and let us get her out of the Family, Mrs. *Hawley*. —To be sure, my *Lady*, said Mrs *Hawley*, who hated *Emily*, because she look'd upon her as her Rival, I shall be proud to oblige your Ladyship. I'll do my best, your Ladyship may depend upon it, for she is a very artful Girl, and my good Mistress is very credulous.—Aye, so my Aunt is, Mrs. *Hawley*, but I muſt watch the Girl's coming out. You won't forget, Mrs. *Hawley*.—Oh dear, my Lady, to be ſure, ſaid the ſmirking Waiting-Gentlewoman, Miſs *Willis* is juſt now gone into the Dreſſing-Room. I'll ſtay in the Chamber: Perhaps I may hear ſomething.

It will not be amiſs to tell the Reader here, why *Emily* was not found in her own Apartment, and why ſhe made Mrs *Freelove* wait ſo long for her. As the Evening was remarkably fine, ſhe had ſtrolled into the Garden, to which however, ſhe was led more from a Principle of Good-nature, than an Inclination to walk (the Seaſon being too far advanced for Walking after Duſk). For a little Dog, of whom Mrs *Freelove* was particularly fond, had by ſome Accident, been ſhut out, and made ſuch a yelping under her Window, that ſhe cou'd not be eaſy without going down and relieving him from his uncomfortable Situation. Juſt as ſhe was going to perform this good-natur'd Action, a ſudden Noiſe in the Garden frighten'd the little Animal ſo much, that he ran away before ſhe got to the Door. But as she thought he was not far off, she ventured a few Steps in Search of him. While she was thus employ'd, her Hand was seiz'd by a Man, whom she cou'd not recollect, and was therefore very much alarm'd: But her Fears were soon remov'd upon Lord *B——*'s speaking to her, though she was greatly vext to be so caught by him.—Don't be surpriz'd, Miss *Willis*, said his Lordship, for 'tis on your Account I am now here. I am not ignorant of any Thing that has passed at *Fenly-Manor* since I left it. I cannot bear to be supplanted by Sir *George.*—Just as he had spoken these Words, one of Mrs. *Freelove*'s Maids appear'd, and told her Message. *Emily* then begg'd Lord *B——* to let her go, with so much Eagerness, that he consented, but not before he had made her promise to let him see her again, telling her he wou'd keep himself conceal'd from the *Family*. *Emily* was forced to grant him his own Terms, in order to get rid of him, and to prevent Mrs. *Freelove*'s waiting for her, whom she wou'd not have disobliged on any Account. The Maid unluckily heard all that passed between *Emily* and his *Lordship*, and took Care to tell Mrs. *Hawley*,

Hawley, (because the Footman had told her she was not so handsome as Miss *Willis*,) who soon convey'd the new Intelligence to Lady *Caroline* and *Prate*, while *Emily* was with her Protectress.

Emily was very gravely received by Mrs. *Freelove*, who soon accosted her in this Manner. I think, *Emily*, said she, I have treated you kindly ever since you have been with me, and endeavoured to make your Situation in my Family agreeable. My own Behaviour, I think, I can answer for, but I will not pretend to answer for the Behaviour of other People —You have, indeed, Madam, said *Emily*, been the kindest, best of Friends to me, and I have led a very happy Life under your generous Protection.—Do you mean as you say, Child? replied Mrs. *Freelove*—I shou'd be very ungrateful, and very unworthy of your Favours, Madam, said *Emily*, extremely surprized at this unusual Preamble, if I meant otherwise.—Why I think you would, said Mrs. *Freelove* But are you sure that you have behaved as well on your Part as I have on mine? Have you never deceived me? Have you never concealed any Thing from me me that has happened to you since you have been with me?—This last Question was a very home one, and made *Emily* blush excessively, not that she imagined she had been guilty of any Crime in concealing her Inclination for Sir *George*, (for she bestowed not a Thought on Lord *B*——, tho' she had just left him) but she was afraid Mrs *Freelove* might be offended with her, if she heard of the Secret from any other Person. It was this Apprehension which filled her Face with Confusion, and made her at a Loss for a ready Answer. Mrs. *Freelove*'s Suspicions were strengthened by these unfavourable Circumstances, and she thus went on.—Your Silence, Child, said she, and that sudden Change of Colour, wou'd make you suspected, if I had no other Proofs of your Folly and Ingratitude; for sure it is the Height of Folly for a Girl of your low Birth and mean Education to pretend to *my* Nephew, and the Height of Ingratitude to me, after my kind Behaviour to you, to think of carrying on such an Intrigue in my House. I aver, when I first heard you accused, I did not believe you were capable of acting so basely; but now your own Countenance,

…enance, Child, condemns you, nor will you, I believe, dare to deny it.

Poor *Emily*, whose Distress and Confusion increased every Moment, was ready to sink into the Ground. She looked as pale as Death, and trembled exceedingly. She could not muster up Courage enough to speak to the Charge against her, she wished to vindicate herself, but she could not bear to accuse her Lover. She knew not what to say. It would be vain, she thought, and foolish, to tell her Benefactress every Thing Sir *George* and Lord *B*—— had said to her by way of Gallantry. As she found, however, that Mrs. *Freelove* expected some Kind of Reply, she, with much Struggling, said, I am very unhappy, Madam, in being suspected by you, of a Crime which I never committed. I am not so ungrateful a Wretch as you take me to be —*Indeed* I am not. I can most faithfully assure you, that I never encouraged the young Gentleman, your Nephew, to treat me otherwise than as your Dependent, nor did I ever imagine he cou'd look on me in any other Light. 'Tis very well, said Mrs. *Freelove*, I was told you would

would deny it, and I find I was told right. But you don't deny it in the Manner I expected and wished for. Go, Child, go into your own Room——— But you must a very little while longer call that Room your own, for I shall not keep you to disturb the Peace of my Family.

Emily was very much shocked at the Conclusion of this Speech, because there was nothing she dreaded so much as the losing Mrs. *Freelove*'s Esteem, which she looked upon as her only Support, for *Hippocrene* had deserted her, and she had received no Letter from Mrs *Easy* for several Months, though she had written to her often. She was, moreover, afraid that her Reputation might suffer, if she was turned out of the Family on Sir *George*'s Account, and therefore endeavoured to soften the old Lady in her Favour. She threw herself at her Feet, with her Eyes streaming, and her Bosom heaving with undissembled Sorrows, and implored her not to turn her out of the Family too hastily. Have a little Patience with me, Madam, said she, inflict what Punishment you think proper on me, I will bear it chearfully, and
applaud

applaud your Goodness, if you will permit me to be near you. Let me be always immur'd in your own Apartment, and never see your Nephew, if you imagine I have had any Transactions with him. But indeed I am falsely accused. —Well, well, said Mrs. *Freelove*, a little moved at her Tears, Sighs, and broken Accents, do as I order you, go to your Chamber, and stay there till I send for you. As she spoke these words in a milder Tone, *Emily* began to be soothed by Hope, and immediately obeyed her Commands. Scarce had she left the Room, when Lord *B*—— unluckily intercepted her. He had been watching for her all the Evening, though she had not the least Suspicion that *he* was the Person on whom she was supposed to have a Design (as Sir *George* was always uppermost in her Thoughts) she deemed it particularly prudent to shun him at that Juncture, and therefore endeavoured to pass by him, telling him that Mrs. *Freelove* had sent her to fetch Something in a Hurry. But Lord *B*—— was too quick-sighted a Lover to be so imposed upon. He soon perceived she had been in Tears, and asked the Cause of them, swearing that he would

would take her Part againſt any Perſon who had offended her, even his Aunt herſelf, and declaring at the ſame Time, that he muſt ſpeak with her that Night, and that he would be put off no longer. *Emily*, frighten'd leſt her ſtaying to talk with Lord *B——* ſhould create new Suſpicions, and longing to retire to give a Looſe to her Griefs, told him ſhe could not poſſibly ſtay, becauſe Mrs. *Freelove* would be angry if ſhe heard he was there without her Knowledge; and begged, if he had the leaſt Regard for her, he would not detain her. Let me but go for the preſent, ſaid ſhe, my Lord, and I will take the firſt Opportunity to give you a Hearing.—Ungrateful *Emily*, replied his Lordſhip, you know too well my Sentiments with regard to you, but Time and your Behaviour will make a Change in them. Sir *George*, Madam, will not be ſo eaſily fooled. *Emily* ſtaid not to make any Reply, but ran directly to her Room, and faſtened the Door.

Mrs *Freelove*, as ſoon as *Emily* left her, had ſummoned Mrs. *Hawley*, by touching her Bell. Mrs *Hawley*, however, was cunning enough not to obey the Summons, till she had heard all that passed between *Emily* and Lord *B——*, whose Motions she watched with a cordial Delight. When she entered the Room, her Mistress said to her, Well, *Hawley*, I have talked with *Emily*, and though she looked very much surprized and confounded, I hope she is not guilty —I don't know, said *Hawley*, what you think, Madam, or what she has told you, but I am sure she has just left Lord *B——*, and I can tell you what they have been talking about. —Just left Lord *B——*, said Mrs. *Freelove*, sure *Hawley* you dream! Why my Nephew is not in the Country Sir *George*, I suppose, you mean —No, no, Madam, said *Hawley*, I mean Lord *B——* He is not known, indeed, to be here, but I can take my Oath I saw him just now in the Gallery with Miss *Willis*, and heard what he said to her; and *Susan*, the Laundry-Maid, saw him with her in the Garden, just when you sent me to fetch her to you —Amazement! said Mrs. *Freelove* Is it possible the Girl can be such a Hypocrite?—O dear, Ma'am, replied *Hawley*, to be sure you have been sadly abused by her, and so I cou'd have told you long ago, but

but Servants must not speak till they are spoken to. O she is a sad little deceitful Hypocrite. Poor Lady *Caroline* has often, with her Eyes brim-full of Tears, pitied you, and said, How it grieves me, Mrs *Hawley*, to see my kind, generous Aunt so grossly imposed upon by such a coquetting Flirt.

Mrs *Freelove* did not relish her Niece's *Pity*. It rouzed her Pride and Indignation, for few People care to have it imagined that they are ever imposed upon, and the Person who pities them, in such a Case, indirectly calls their Understanding in Question, and who can bear an Affront to their Understandings? We have all a Spice of Vanity in us, and cannot chuse to be thought deficient in Sagacity. Nay, I believe, the major Part of Mankind wou'd rather have their *Morals* than their *Intellects* suspected. Mrs. *Freelove* was a very good Sort of Woman, when Pride was out of the Way. But she valued herself not a little on account of her Penetration, and was therefore stung to the Quick by this artful Speech of Mrs. *Hawley*'s.—I am resolved, said she, with some Vehemence, to sift this Affair

Affair to the bottom. I will know the Truth, if it is possible. Call the Girl to me this Instant, and send Somebody to look for Lord *B——*. *Hawley* obeyed the first Part of this Message with great Punctuality, but did not pay so much Regard to the latter Part of it, because she feared his Lordship was too much *Emily*'s Friend to be a proper Person to appear before her Lady at this critical Juncture. This Apprehension made her return to her Lady, and tell her, that my Lord was not to be found. And herein she told a Truth, though unknowingly; for his Lordship, vext at *Emily*'s abrupt Departure from him, and thinking that his Aunt would discover his Designs, if he should be found lurking about the House, left *Fanly-Manor* in a Quarter of an Hour after *Emily* retired to her Apartment.

Emily received Mrs *Freelove*'s second Message with a slight Satisfaction, being in hopes that she had changed her Mind in her Favour. But she soon found she had been too sanguine; for as soon as she entered the Dressing-Room, Mrs *Freelove* thus accosted her—I wonder, Child, you are not ashamed to look me in the Face, after having uttered such notorious Falsehoods. Will you dare to deny that you have seen Lord *B——* twice this Evening alone?—*Emily* received this second Rebuff with as little Composure as she did the first, but was secretly rejoiced, however, to find that no Mention was made of Sir *George*, and answered without Hesitation, I *have seen Lord B——*, Madam, twice this Evening, but I neither knew of his coming to the House, nor staid to converse with him.——No, said Mrs. *Freelove*, no longer, I suppose, than it served your Purpose; but I know every Thing you said to him, and for that Reason, and for your audacious Behaviour, you shall leave this House early in the Morning.—*Emily* was quite Thunder-struck at this severe Resolution, and would fain have endeavoured to plead her Innocence, but this unlucky Circumstance was too strong against her. The old Lady, though she always piqued herself on keeping up her Dignity, even when she was in a Passion, almost lost it at the Sight of a Girl whom she thought had been guilty of the highest Ingratitude. She ordered her to leave the Room, but told her she should be narrowly watched

till

till the next Morning, and that the Stage-Coach should then convey her to *London.* *Emily*, finding that Mrs *Freelove* was too much inflamed against her to hear Reason, once more returned to her Apartment with a chearless Countenance, and a heavy Heart.

Lady *Caroline*, who, from a Room adjoining, had observed every Look, and heard every Word that passed between *Emily* and her *Aunt*, went to the latter as soon as she knew she was alone, in tip-top Spirits, because her Scheme had succeeded, with a Design to spend the Remainder of the Evening with her, for fear she should relent. Mrs *Freelove*, pleased with her Niece's Complaisance and good-humour'd Behaviour, kept her to Supper in her Dressing-Room.

During these Transactions, Sir *George* was absent from *Fanly-M——.* He was gone to spend the Evening with a neighbouring Gentleman, from whom he found a pressing Card, on his Return from the Airing with his Aunt and *Emily.* He would have been very glad to decline the Invitation on *Emily*'s Account, but cou'd not handsomely, as he was intreated to meet several Friends just arrived from *London*, and to stay all Night.

Lady *Caroline*'s Joy was considerably increased, when she found that Sir *George* was to stay all Night with his Neighbour, being in Hopes that, as he was not an early Riser, he would not return the next Morning to *Fairly-Manor* till *Emily* was far enough out of the Way. Her Hopes were not frustrated; for the *Coach*, which was to carry *Emily* from all she loved and valued, appeared very early at the Gate.

Poor *Emily* wept bitterly at the Sight of the Stage-Coach, and beseech'd Mrs. *Hawley* with the utmost Earnestness, to let her see Mrs. *Freelove* before she went into it. But the Waiting-Gentlewoman hated her so thoroughly, that she was deaf to her Request. As for Mis *Freelove*, she wou'd not trust herself with a last Interview, for fear she shou'd be melted to Compassion, and induced to act contrary to the Honour of her antient and noble Family. Lady *Caroline* stuck close to her Aunt, to keep her from

from wavering, as well as to shew her Contempt for a poor low-born Wretch, who dared to think of *her* Brother. So that *Emily* was only attended by the Servants, who all loved her (except *Hawley* and *Susan*) and parted from her with the greatest Reluctance, and wished her better Fortune. *Emily* thanked them for their kind Wishes, bid them civilly adieu, and told the Coachman she was ready to set off.

END of the SECOND BOOK.

EMILY WILLIS:

OR, THE

HISTORY

OF A

NATURAL DAUGHTER.

BOOK III

AS there was nobody in the Coach but a young Woman, who made no Appearance, and her Child, she did not endeavour to conceal her Affliction, which was, indeed, very great on many Accounts. She was in a Manner turn'd out of Doors by a Lady of Fashion, who had once shewed a great Regard for her; she was going to a Family who had disliked her, who had endeavour'd to impose upon her, and who were disgust-
ing.

ing to her for several Reasons. She was vext to be torn away from a Man whose winning Behaviour had made an Impression on her tender Heart; and she was full of Apprehensions that even her Friend Mrs *Easy* had forsaken her, because she had not, for a long Time, receiv'd an, Letter from her Whilst she was at *Fairy-Manor*, she thought too much on Sir *George*, to think much of any body else but now the Neglect of Mrs *Easy* pain'd her with double Force. The Loss of her Lover wou'd have been enough to fill her with Melancholy, without any additional Disappointment; but such a Train of Vexations distress'd her so much, that she was just ready to faint away The young Woman in the Coach, who had herself a very disconsolate Air, perceiving a sudden Paleness to overspread her Fellow-Traveller's Face, thus addressed her, with a great deal of Humanity I am afraid, Miss, said she, you are very ill, and want some Help. I wish it was in my Power to assist you, for you seem to be quite opprest with Sorrow: And indeed, continued she, with tearful Eyes, I am unhappy myself, but I have been long so, and may be better able to bear Hardships than you,

you, who seem to have but lately met with them. But don't give Way to Grief, Miss, your Case perhaps is not so desperate as mine. As she spoke these Words in a gentle, pitying Tone, *Emily* thank'd her for her Obligingness, and told her she found herself better, and wou'd try to follow her Advice.

Emily found great Satisfaction in this young Woman's Company. Not that she was pleased to meet with one of her own Sex as unhappy as herself (for she was always disposed to sympathize with the Unfortunate) but there was a Something infinitely soothing in the Melancholy of this Companion, and in the Concern she discovered for her. *Emily* in Return, express'd the same Concern for *her*, took Notice of the little Girl she had in her Lap, and ask'd her several Questions. The pretty Prattler answer'd her Questions with a smiling Face, and said, Mamma and I are going to see Papa— Does your Papa then live in *London*, my Dear? said *Emily*. —O Miss, said the Mother, bursting into Tears, that Man, that Child's Father, and my Husband, has left us, I fear, for ever! —But why shou'd you give yourself up to Defpair, Madam? faid *Emily*, I hope you are miftaken, I hope your Fears are groundlefs; becaufe I can hardly fuppofe that a Man wou'd quit fo agreeable a Wife, and fo fweet a little Daughter, except they had greatly offended him, which I do not think to be your Cafe —No, indeed, Mifs, faid fhe, I never defignedly offended him, even in Thought; but if you will condefcend to hear me with Patience, I will tell you how I came to be thus miferable. I know it is not good Manners to trouble every body with one's Afflictions, but as you are no Stranger to Sorrow yourfelf, you will excufe me And as you are young and handfome, my Story may be of fome Service to you.

I am the Daughter of a Farmer in *Kent*, who was for many Years in very good Circumftances, and able to give me, what was thought in the Country, a good Education I was fent betimes to a great Boarding-School, and there learnt every Thing but Mufick and *French* with the reft of the Scholars. At Fifteen my Mother defired to have me Home, and employed me chiefly in Needle-work, 'till her Death, which
happened

happened about three Years afterwards I then kept my Father's House 'till I was One-and-Twenty, at which Time he died and left me but thirty Pounds, having met with great Losses for the two last Years of his Life. As I could not think of subsisting long on so small a Sum, I determined to go to Service, and made Enquiries for an Upper-Maid's Place. In a short Time, a young Lady, who had been my School-fellow, accidentally came into *Kent*, and made me an Offer of living with her as her Companion. I the more readily accepted her Offer, because I thought she was remarkably good-humour'd. She was left an Orphan, like myself, only possest of a very handsome Fortune. She took me to *London* with her, made me several genteel Presents, that I might be fit to attend her in the many Visits she paid and receiv'd, and introduced me to several Female Cousins, who treated me very politely. She had an only Brother, who had an Estate of eight Hundred a Year in *Oxfordshire*, where, before I came to *London*, he commonly resided, only spending a Month or two with his Sister in the Depth of Winter. This Gentleman soon took a Fancy to me,

and soon let me know his Mind; for his Sister, who had no Suspicions about him, often left us together He endeavoured many Ways to prevail with me to be his Mistress, but when he found I was absolutely deaf to all his Solicitations, and that I threatened to leave his Sister, if he persisted to worry me, he changed his Mind, and offered to marry me. I freely confess, I was delighted with this Proposal, for he was so agreeable a Man, I cou'd not look on him with Indifference: And I flattered myself that his Sister and Cousins were too much my Friends to object to our Union. He told me the Marriage must be performed privately, for particular Reasons, and be kept secret for some Time. I comply'd with his Request, but took Care to have proper Witnesses and a Certificate In short, we were married, and I thought myself the happiest Creature in the World by being his Wife; having, as I imagined, gain'd a most amiable, indulgent Husband, and made my Fortune. But alas! I was only contriving my own Ruin. We kept our Marriage conceal'd, 'till I was too near lying-in to hide it any longer. His Sister first discover'd my Condition, and
then

then fufpected me of being her Brother's Miftrefs. But when I, with his Leave, told her we were married, I thought fhe wou'd have run diftracted. No Words can exprefs the Rage fhe flew into. She, who was fo fond of me before, now loaded me with the bittereft Reproaches. Nor was I alone the Object of her Fury, her Brother too underwent a very fevere Lecture, which fhe concluded by telling him, that fince he had ruin'd both his Character and Fortune, fhe begg'd he wou'd take his Trull of a Wife Home with him, for fhe fhou'd no longer ftay in her Houfe. He fired, and I think with Reafon, at this monftrous Behaviour, and we quitted the Houfe immediately. He took a Lodging for me in the Neighbourhood, in which I was foon deliver'd of this Daughter, with whom he then feem'd highly delighted, and endeavoured to reconcile his Family to me; but he tried in vain. His Sifter incens'd all his Relations fo much againft us both, that I cou'd not ftir out without being infulted either by them, or their Servants, whom they order'd to affront me where-ever they met me. My Hufband, fhock'd at this Treatment, brought me down into this County,

(Nor-

(*Northamptonshire*) and took Lodgings for me at a Farm House, not caring to carry me to his own Estate, for Fear his Sister should pursue us even to *that* Place. In this Retreat we lived a Twelvemonth. He then left me (pretending that Business call'd him to Town) and my little *Betsy*, who just began to lisp the Name of Papa, with some Money, and Directions where to write to him, tho', he said, he shou'd stay no longer than two Months at farthest. I parted from him with true Sorrow, for I loved him dearly; and still love him, tho' he cruelly neglects me. It is now almost a Year and a Half since he took Leave of me. I have wrote to him constantly during that Time, once a Week, but received no Letter from him after the first Month of his Absence. I am now going to *London*, in Search of him, and shou'd have set out sooner, had I not been afraid of offending him, knowing he dreads nothing so much as my falling in the Way of his Relations. But Necessity is now added to my other Motives. My Money, though I managed it with the greatest Frugality, has been spent some Time, and I have no Hopes of a Supply, for I cannot bear to ask the good People

People with whom I lodge, to trust me any longer. I am therefore going to enquire after my Husband, in Hopes that the Sight of a Woman and a Child, whom he once fondly doated on, may soften his Heart to Pity, and make him desirous to relieve our Necessities. But I fear my Journey will be in vain. If it proves so, I shall not know which Way to turn myself, nor how to provide for myself and my dear Child.—Here the young Woman ended her Narrative, with a fresh Torrent of Tears. *Emily* sincerely sympathized with her, and said all she cou'd to comfort her, but did not think it necessary to make a Discovery of herself and her own Affairs.

When they stopt to dine at the Inn, *Emily* intreated her Companion to eat with her, and insisted on discharging the whole Reckoning herself. In this Manner did she act at Supper, and at Breakfast, and Dinner the next Day, for she found that the poor Woman had little more than sufficient to pay her own Passage and the Child's; though she appeared not to know her Circumstances. When they arrived at their Journey's End,

End, they parted with that Kind of Sorrow which Persons naturally feel, on a Recollection of their own Distresses. *Emily* got into a Hackney-coach, with her Bundles, and ordered the Coachman to drive directly to Mr *Hippocrene*'s.

As soon as she was alone, she again ruminated on every Thing that had happened to her. Her Companion's Story gave Rise to many Reflections. Suppose, said she to herself, I had accepted Lord B————'s Offer of Marriage?—— Suppose, Sir *George* had honoured me with the same Offer?——Might I not have experienced the same ill Treatment from his Family, as this poor Woman has met with from her Husband's Relations, and have made both him and myself miserable? And could I have borne to see the Man I fondly loved, miserable on my Account? No, certainly. Besides, how much more unhappy is this poor Creature, by having a helpless Babe to provide for? I have only myself to take Care of: I can get my Living any where, should I be reduced to Difficulties. Let me therefore forget Sir *George:* let me banish him,

amiable

amiable as he is, from my Remembrance. And since the Intimacies, tho' ever so innocent, of *his* Sex, are so fatal to *mine*, let me for the future avoid all Connection with Men.—But, alas! there is as little Stability in Female Friendships; else why has Mrs *Easy* deserted me? I was at too great a Distance to have offended her, and she cannot have yet heard of my Disgrace. Mrs. *Freelove* too, after all her Kindness to me, has given me up. But, I suppose her Family-Pride got the better of her friendly Disposition. Just as she had finished this Soliloquy, the Coach stopp'd at Mr *Hippocrene*'s Door, about the Beginning of a clear, cold Evening in *February*; but how great was her Surprize to see both the Shop and House shut up! While she was staring full of Wonder, Mr. *Hippocrene*'s next Neighbour, who stood at his Shop-door, told her, that all the Family were gone to *Ireland*. If you will walk into my House, Miss, said Mr. *Metal*, (for he had long known her) I will inform you what I have heard about the Poet: for by that Name was *Hippocrene* distinguished in the Neighbourhood. *Emily*, who did not know where to go, thanked him

him for his Civility, and accepted his Offer.

Mr. *Metal* was, by Trade, a Brazier, and by dint of Industry had acquired a handsome Fortune, but he unluckily married, in the Midst of his Affluence, a Woman of an expensive Turn, and was now barely able to make both Ends meet. Mrs *Metal* was the Daughter of a Butcher in St. *James*'s Market, and valued herself not a little on her personal Beauty; for which, indeed, her Husband chiefly made his Addresses to her, having a great Propensity to handsome Women. She had an immoderate Fondness for Dress, and was always aiming to copy the Modes and Manners of People of Fashion. These ruling Passions gave her Husband many uneasy Moments. She had contracted her Affectation of Quality by keeping Company with Ladies Women, and Noblemens Gentlemen, who flattered her, in order to have the Liberty of eating and drinking at her House whenever they were out of Place, or had no where else to go.

Mrs. *Metal* was also doatingly fond of two Daughters, her only Children, because, with a little of her Beauty, they inherited a great deal of her Taste for Dress and Extravagance. These Girls were, at the Time of *Emily*'s Arrival which happened to be on a *Saturday*, very busy in preparing Ornaments to make a Figure with the next Day at their Parish-Church, which they never fail'd to frequent, in order to shew their fine Cloaths, and their fine Airs, to excite the Envy of all their Female Neighbours, and to attract the Admiration of all the young Fellows. They had, however, no other Design on the male Part of the Congregation, than to inspire half a Dozen Danglers with a hopeless Passion for them, which might end in hanging, drowning, &c. for they had much better Notions of Life, than to think of marrying their Equals, and of setting down comfortably in a housewifely Way, as their Grand-mothers had done before them.

Mr. *Metal*, knowing how importantly his Daughters were employed, and not daring to disturb them, conducted *Emily* into a small Room behind the Shop,

Shop, in which his Wife was condescending to make a Pigeon-Pye for their *Sunday*'s Dinner, but which she huddled out of the Way as fast as she could, (not chusing to be catch'd in performing so menial an Office) and saluted her new Visitor with great Civility, and gave her a hearty Welcome to *London*, (for she supposed that *Emily* was only come to Town for a Day or two, as she had heard from Mrs. *Hippocrene*, whom she used to visit, that she was gone to be a Companion to a Lady of Quality) La! Miss *Willis*, said she, are you not vastly surpriz'd to hear that Mr. *Hippocrene*'s Family is gone away from this Part of the World?—Yes, indeed, Madam, said *Emily*, I am vastly surprized, and should be glad to know the Reason of their Departure —The Reason Miss, replied Mr. *Metal*, is this· You must know he had composed a Play, which he said was a very fine one· And so, to be sure, it might be for aught I know, for I don't pretend to be a Judge of those Matters, not I, tho' by the Way, I'm afraid my poor Neighbour's Brain was a little crack'd: But that's not to my Business He thought he should make Money of his Piece, it seems,

which

which to tell you the Truth, I believe he very much wanted—So what does he do but carry it to the Master of *Drury-Lane* Playhouse, who told him it wou'dn't do, and advised him to take it Home and new write it, but he was obstinate and woudn't: So he carries it to the Master of the other House, but he refused it too, so my poor Neighbour was almost distracted, and flew into a violent Passion, and said they were all a Pack of Fools, and did not know a good Play from a bad one. So he sold off his Stock in Trade, for a small Matter of ready Money, and set off in a Huff for *Ireland*, where he said he doubted not but his Play wou'd be well receiv'd with the greatest Applause — Is he then gone to settle in *Ireland*, Sir? said *Emily*.—Why I am afraid, Miss, said *Metal*, with an arch Grin, that he will never settle any where, but I hope your Money is safe?—Indeed I can't tell, said *Emily*. I have not received a Letter since I went into the Country, and don't in the least know how to dispose of myself, for I fully expected to find the Family where I left them —Why, if that's the Case, Miss, you are very welcome to stay a Week or a Fortnight with

with me, and you can turn yourself about, as they say—If you will take up your Lodging with my Daughter *Poll*.—Lard, Mr *Metal*, said his Lady, will you never understand yourself? Your Daughter is now of a proper Age to be called Miss *Metal*: *Poll* sounds so *vulgar*, and besides is so like a Parrot, that I can't endure it.—Well, well, said the good Man, I don't stand on such nice Distinctions, not I, but most Wives know more than their Husbands, now-a-Days. We shall all grow wiser, in Time, my Dear; the World is prodigiously enlightened in this Age. But come, call down *Miss Metal*, since you will have it so, and let Miss *Bet Metal* come with her Sister *Miss Metal*.—This Request was uttered so much in the Imperative Mood, that Mrs *Metal*, who was not accustomed to Obedience, did not relish it. However, she only gave her Spouse a gentle Frown, and said, she supposed they would come when they had a Fancy for it.—Aye, said *Metal*, but methinks it wou'd be but civil in them to come and welcome my pretty Guest here. But, however, since the *Young Ladies*, said he, with a Sneer, are not to be disturb'd, we will do as well as we can

without

without them. *Emily* desired she might not put his Family to any Inconvenience. I'll stay, if you please, Sir, said she, To-night, because it is too late to look for a Lodging, but, I hope, I shan't be troublesome any longer.——Poo, poo, said *Metal*, never talk of that, Miss, you are as welcome as if you were my own Child. Besides, To-morrow's *Sunday*, and you can't well take a Lodging till next Week.—But perhaps, said Mrs. *Metal*, Miss *Wills* may have some Friends she may chuse to see while she stays in Town. It is not good Manners, my Dear, to importune People, but when you are once set upon a Thing, you are always so teazing. I suppose, *Miss*, said she to *Emily*, you came up in my Lady's Coach, and that it will carry you down again? *Emily* blushed and sighed at this Question, but mustered up her Spirits as well as she could, and said, I can't tell when I shall leave *London*, Madam, Mr. *Hippocrene*'s abrupt Departure will, in all Probability, make a great Alteration in my Affairs.—Just as Mrs. *Metal* was going to make a Reply to this Speech, the two young Ladies entered the Room.

As

As these young Ladies never had much Acquaintance with *Emily* (for their Mother had always cautioned them against being too intimate with handsome young Women, for Reasons which will hereafter appear) they only saluted her in a cold, formal Manner. When the frigid Salutation was over, Miss *Metal* presented an immense Gauze Ruff to her Mother, with about an Ell of scarlet Ribbon dangling to it, and cried, Dear *Mamma*, do but see how pretty it is! it will become me vastly, won't it?—Well, but said the Father, winking at *Emily*, you might have left *us* to have said that, Miss.—Pray be quiet Mr. *Metal*, said his Wife, you are always finding Fault with you don't know what —She was here interrupted by the Appearance of a dirty, ill-looking Drab, who served her and her polite Family in the Capacity of a Servant.—*Alice*, said she to the Maid, lay the Cloth for Supper in the Dining-Room. *Alice* told her that the Dining-room was not dry, having been scour'd since Dinner.—Aye, said she, this it is to keep such a Snail about the House. Don't I always order the Room to be cleaned in the Morning, that it may be ready for Company? But it will never be otherwife till we keep a Footman, and fo I often tell Mr. *Metal*. I hope, Mifs *Willis*, you will excufe it.— Come, come, no more Apologies, Wife, faid Mr. *Metal*, let the Cloth be laid fomewhere, I dare fay, Mifs *Willis* will be glad to pick a Bit after her Journey, and I am fure my Stomach has been cioaking this half Hour.—Dear Mr *Metal*, how you talk, faid his Lady, do People of any Fafhion go to Supper at Fight o'Clock? I dare fay Mifs *Willis* has not been ufed to fuch *vulgar* Hours. But if you don't know what to do with yourfelf, go to your Compting-Houfe, we can divert ourfelves with our own Chat, I warrant you.

While the Cloth was laying for Supper, which was in about an Hour after, the Daughters defired *Emily* to ftep with them into another Room, and give her Opinion of a new-fafhion'd Cap. They were no fooner withdrawn, than Mr. *Metal* afked his Wife which of his Daughters Mifs *Willis* was to lie with?—With neither, faid fhe haftily.—Hey-day, faid he, where the Devil then?—Why with *Alice* to be fure, faid fhe, where elfe would you have her lie? Do you

you think think *my* Daughters shall be parted to make Room for *your* Visitors?——With *Alice!* that she sha'nt, by G—d, said he, what, put the Friend, nay, almost Child of my next Neighbour, with that dirty Bunter? No, no, let the three Girls pig together for once, or if they are not small enough for one Bed, why turn one of our own up Stairs—No, indeed, said his Lady, with an imperious Tone, I assure you I think my Daughters far above any Body in this House, except ourselves, therefore since you have taken such a Fancy to Strangers, to the Prejudice of your own Children, let her lie in the spare Bed in the Garret, next to the Maid's.—Here the Appearance of Supper, and of the Girls, put an End to their Altercation for a Time. Soon after Supper *Emily*, who was heartily tired both with her Journey and Company, desired they would shew her where she was to lie — The young Ladies very readily offered to conduct her to her Bed-chamber, and left their Papa and Mamma to enjoy their own Conversation.

Mr *Metal* opened the Dialogue (while his Wife sat in a glouting Mood) by saying, laying, Upon my Word, I think Miss *Willis* is mightily improved, and grows a very handsome young Woman—I can't see any Beauty in her, said his Lady, but you're always finding People handsome out of your own Family, and neglect those who are in it.—Not I, by *Jove*, said he, but I can see as well as other Folks, thank God, my Eyes were not given me for nothing. I think she is very pretty, and am sorry you and your Daughters looked so damn'd shy on her.—Why, how the Devil wou'd you have us look, Mr *Metal*, said his Lady, on a Girl, who may be come for aught we know, to take the Bread out of our Mouths? You know I hate to encourage young Girls that are tolerable, till our own are well settled. To what Purpose have I, do you think, bred your Daughters like Gentlewomen, but that they might make their Fortunes like the Miss what-d'ye-callums?—Pshaw, Pshaw, said *Metal*, that's building Castles in the Air indeed. Why *Poll* and *Bet* are nothing to compare to them. The Girls are straight, I grant you, and not much scar'd by the Small-pox, but as for any Thing else, they are but so so, and, I believe, if they are to make

Vol. I.   I   their

their Fortunes by their Beauty, they will stay long enough ⸺ It will be your Fault if they don't make their Fortunes, Mr. *Metal*, said she, for you are always thrusting Somebody under their Nose. Don't you remember how you brought Miss *Prudence*, the Country Curate's Daughter to Town, just as *Molly* was trying to draw in young Doctor *Smalbrains?* and don't you remember that she carried him off too? ⸺Nay, nay, said *Metal*, I'm sure she has no Catch. He is a poor walking Doctor, who has not above half a dozen Patients; and I'd rather see my Daughter in the Bar of an Ale-house, than married to such a Glyster-pipe ⸺O fie for Shame, Mr. *Metal*, said she, hold your foolish Tongue. Mr *Smalbrains* is a very good Doctor, and will come to have a great deal of Business, by-and-bye. If he had married *Molly*, with her Fortune, they wou'd soon have set up a Chariot, I warrant you ⸺I say Fortune, cried *Metal*, pray who the Devil is she to have it from?⸺Why, who shou'd she have it from, said Mrs. *Metal*, but from her Father?⸺From me? By G⸺d I can't give her a Sous, not I ⸺Not give your Children Fortunes, Mr *Metal?* said

said she.—No, indeed, replied he, you spend every Farthing I get in Ribbons, Laces, and Tuncum-Tiancums. You have it all among you, faith.—Then since 'tis so, said Mrs *Metal*, boiling with Passion, you ought not to bring People into the House, to eat up your poor Wife's and Children's Substance.—Fie, fie, *Sally*, don't expose yourself so; prythee, don't.—No, Sir, but I'll expose *you* before I have done. What, I warrant this Minx is a Mistress of yours, and that's the Reason you are so much afraid of her. I'll lay my Life 'tis so. But she shall troop To-morrow Morning: I'll send her packing, a Hussy—I'll have no Wenches brought here, I assure you, Mr *Metal*. I'll teach you to bring your handsome young Sluts here. A fine Thing indeed!—Mr *Metal*, finding that his Lady grew very warm towards the Conclusion of this Speech, and not caring to have his Rest disturb'd for the Remainder of the Evening, (for disturb'd he knew it wou'd certainly be if he did not make a proper Submission) thus replied.—Why, *Sally*, why all this Heat about Nothing? I meant no Harm in asking the Girl to stay with us till she cou'd provide herself with a

I 2   Lodging

Lodging I know no more of her than you do ---Stay with us? said Mrs *Metal*, stay here? very fine, indeed! What ask you don't know who, you don't know what? No, no, she shan't stay here, I'll take Care of that I *will* be Mistress in my own House, I warrant. Bring such a Creature h.re? Why, she may be a Whore or a Thief for any Thing I know.——Aye, or for any Thing *I* know, my Dear, said *Metal*; but I thought she was an honest Person, or you may be sure I shou'dn't have been so civil to her.---*You* thought, replied his Lady, and what signifies your thinking? It never comes to any Good, I am sure Not to save Fortunes for your Children? Go, you shabby Fellow, I'm quite asham'd of you ---Why, my Love, said *Metal*, dryly, I thought you always designed the Girls shou'd make their Fortunes, like the Miss what d'ye callums; and, then you know, there was no Occasion for me to trouble my Head about them ---Aye, so I hope they will, for all *you* do all you can to hinder them I'm sure they are thought handsomer by some People, and their bringing up has been better a great deal There's Miss *Metal* is as like me as she can

can ftare, and I'm sure my Beauty was never disputed. I might have made my Fortune over and over, only I was such a bewitch'd Simpleton as to take up with a Noodle of a Brazier. But I am rightly serv'd ——— *Metal*, who was naturally disposed to be quiet after Supper, seeing no End to his Lady's Anger, made no Reply, but seizing a Candle, marched directly to Bed, leaving his loquacious Rib to finish her Ravings by herself.

Poor *Emily*, who had burst into Tears on being left in a miserable Garret, threw herself on the Bed (not caring to go between a Pair of dirty Sheets) and gave way to her own melancholy Reflections. *Hippocrene*'s Departure increas'd the Anguish of her Heart, because she knew not whom to apply to for Subsistence. She determin'd, however, to step in the Morning to Mrs. *Easy*'s Lodgings, and learn what she cou'd about her from her Maid. What other Course to take, she knew not, for she had no Friend to consult, and the Reception she met with where she was, deterr'd her from going any where else. She spent the greatest Part of the Night in Sorrow and Suspence, in Sighs and in Tears, but the Fatigue of her Body, added to that of her Mind, at last lulled her to Rest.

At Ten o'clock in the Morning, Miss *Betsy Metal* wak'd *Emily*. She was sent by her Mother to know if she wou'd come down to Breakfast?

Emily, surprized to find it so late, immediately arose, and attended Miss *Betsy* to the Breakfast-Room, where she told Mrs *Metal*, she wou'd go when the Church Service was ended, and enquire after a Lady of her Acquaintance, with whose Apartments she believed she cou'd make free, till she heard from Mr. *Hippocrene*.

When *Emily* went, after Church, to Mrs *Easy*'s Lodgings, she found Nobody at Home, except an old Woman who cou'd give no Account either of Mrs *Easy* or her *Maid*: But told her she wou'd find her Mistress at Home if she wou'd call again in the Evening. *Emily* was now more puzzled than ever. She was very loth to return to the *Metals*, but cou'd not think of rambling about for Lodgings on a *Sunday*, and, besides, wanted to return the Obligations she thought she was under to these People, for taking her into their House when she was quite at a Loss. She therefore went back again, and gave Miss *Betsy* a very pretty blue Gauze Handkerchief, with a Blond Lace (which had been made for herself by Mrs. *Freelove*'s Orders) and desired Mrs *Metal* to accept of a very handsome Fan for her eldest Daughter. These Presents made Mrs. *Metal* so extremely good-humour'd, that she over-power'd the Donor of them with Expressions of Civility.---Indeed, Miss *Willis*, said she, I insist upon your staying here all Night. You shall lie in our Lodger's Room, Miss *Willis*, for he is out of Town.--I thank you, Madam, for your kind Offer, said *Emily*, but I hope to find my Friend at Home in the Evening, that I may give you no farther Trouble. After this Exchange of Compliments they all dined, in the Dining-Room, on the Pigeon-Pye.

Emily, soon after the Cloth was taken away, set out again to Mrs. *Easy*'s Lodgings, and luckily found the Mistress of the House at Home, who told her she

had

had not heard from Mrs. *Eafy* since she left her, but that her Maid, (whom she had given Leave to go and see her Friends) came frequently to know if her Mistress was returned. *Emily* thanked her for her Intelligence, and said, Pray, Madam, have you a Room to let in your House? No, Madam, said she.—I am very sorry for it, reply'd *Emily*, since I am very desirous of lodging in this Neighbourhood. don't you know of any body who has an Apartment to spare in it?—There is a very pretty neat Room, up Two Pair of Stairs, said she, at the Corner of the Street. but I am not acquainted with the Mistress of the House. However, Miss, my Servant shall wait on you there in the Morning, if you chuse it.—I am much obliged to you, Madam, said *Emily*, but can't you spare her To-night? for I should be glad to leave the Place I at present lodge at, directly.—Yes, Miss, I can spare her, and she shall wait on you in five Minutes. *Emily* again thank'd her for her Civility, and not a little pleased, stepp'd away to Mrs. *Bond*, who shewed her a Room which she liked very well, and agreed to take it, if she might be suffer'd to occupy it that Night. Mrs. *Bond*

Bond made no Objection to her Requeſt. She hired therefore a Coach directly, took Leave of the *Metals*, after returning them many Thanks for their friendly Behaviour to her, pack'd up her Bundles, and returned to her new Apartment.

When *Emily* was a little ſettled in her new Lodging, ſhe began to think what ſhe muſt do for a Subſiſtence till Mrs *Eaſy* returned to Town, (who, ſhe flattered herſelf, would give her Advice) or till Mr *Hippocrene* could be compelled to pay her her Money. Needlework ſhe had been moſt accuſtomed to, and therefore went on the *Monday* Morning (after having paſt a very reſtleſs Night) to Mrs *Coleman*, her Friend's Landlady, and deſired her to recommend her to ſome Plain-work — This Mrs. *Coleman* was a good Sort of Woman, and was acquainted with many reputable Families, from whom ſhe without Difficulty obtained Promiſes to employ *Emily* when they had any Thing in her Way to be done. Mrs *Bond*, to whom *Emily* applied alſo, ſoon brought her half a Dozen Shirts to make for a Gentleman of her Acquaintance

When *Emily* had been only two Days at this new Employment, she received the following Letter from Sir *George:*

To Miss *WILLIS.*

"WORDS are too faint, my dear
" Miss *Willis*, to express the
" Anxiety I have suffered ever since
" your Departure from *Fairly Manor.*
" I shou'd not have left the House as
" I did, if I had suspected that any
" malicious Designs were carrying on
" against you, till I had prevailed on
" my Aunt to do you Justice, and pu-
" nish your false Accusers. When I
" came Home, I found how you had
" been abused, and found also, to my
" Sorrow, that I could be of no Service
" to you, for your Accusers had taken
" the Advantage of your Absence, and
" prejudiced my Aunt entirely against
" *me* as well as *you.* I can faithfully af-
" sure you, that I have tried every Me-
" thod to soften her in Favour of one
" so very deserving her Friendship, as
"   I am

"I am sensible you are, but I have yet
"had no Success.——As soon as I re-
"turned Home, which was about an
"Hour after you set off to *London*, I
"ordered my Servant to mount directly,
"in order to overtake, and never to lose
"Sight of you till I came to Town,
"which was Yesterday —— I would
"have waited on you immediately my-
"self, had I not been afraid of sur-
"prizing you too much. But now you
"know I am so near you, give me
"Leave, I entreat you most earnestly,
"my charming *Emily*, to enjoy the
"sweet Satisfaction of seeing you.—Let
"me persuade you to listen to the Dic-
"tates of a Heart, filled with the
"most sincere and tender Passion for
"you, and which vows to be yours
"alone for ever. I am excessively dis-
"tressed, my lovely Girl, when I reflect
"on the Difficulties you must have met
"with, and cannot bear the Thought
"of your pursuing the Way of Life
"you are in at present, which is every
"Way so far beneath a Woman of
"your Sense, Beauty and Education.
"I have formed a Plan for your future
"Happiness, which I hope I shall pre-
"vail on you to agree to ——If you

"comply with it, the whole Study of
"my Life shall be to gratify all your
"Wishes—But before I have your Per-
"mission to wait on you, let me intreat
"you to accept of the inclosed Trifle,
"and to believe me, with the utmost
"Sincerity,

"*Your most Faithful*

"*and Humble Servant,*

"G. FREELOVE"

This Billet-doux was delivered to *Emily* by the Maid of the House, who told her a Servant in a blue Livery waited for an Answer. As *Blue* was the Colour of Mrs. *Freelove*'s Livery, and as the Letter was not directed in Sir *George*'s Hand, she flattered herself that it might come from that Lady by *her* Order, and therefore opened it without hesitating.

As soon as she had opened it, a Bank Note for 500*l*. dropt out, which she picked up immediately, with no small Confusion, and desired the Maid to tell the

the Servant who brought the Letter, that she would answer it in a few Minutes.—She recognized Sir *George*'s Hand, and felt a Tremor from Head to Foot, at the Sight of it. But she soon mustered up Resolution enough to pen the following Reply.

" *To Sir* GEORGE FREELOVE, *Bart.*

" S I R,

" I THINK myself very much obliged
" to you, for endeavouring to vin-
" dicate my Conduct to Mrs. *Freelove*,
" whom I never knowingly offended,
" and whose Favours I shall always
" gratefully acknowledge But as a
" Correspondence of any Kind with
" you, would not only greatly increase
" that Lady's ill Opinion of me, but
" be highly prejudicial to us both, I
" must beg Leave to decline it.—I
" must also beg Leave to return the
" Inclosed, because it must not be
" accepted

" *By, Your Humble Servant,*

" E. W."

Emi'y

Emily folded up this Letter hastily, rung for the Maid, and desired her to give it to the Servant who waited for it: But desired her at the same Time, to say she was not at Home, if he came again, because she was determined not to receive any more Letters from him. The Maid stared her full in the Face, at hearing this Message, but thought fit to deliver both the Letter and the Message to Sir *George*'s Servant, who immediately carried them to his Master.

While the Maid was gone down with her Dispatches, *Emily* had Time to recover a little from the Flutter she had been in. Though she was very much shocked at the Letter she had received, and though she had answered it with so much Spirit and Resolution, she cou'd not help reading it over and over, and dwelling with some Satisfaction on the Lines of a Man who (in Spite of his Designs against her) had made too strong an Impression on her gentle Heart to be easily effaced. Why will he, said she to herself, continue to pursue me?— Can it be only to gratify a brutal Passion? Or, am I really as agreeable in his Eyes as he would make me believe I am?

am? If I *am* agreeable in his Eyes, and if he loves me truly, why will he still seek me only on Terms which I cannot listen to?——But suppose he would make me his Wife against the Consent of all his Relations—I have already determined never to agree to the Match— What should I then do?—Forget him for ever, except he and his Family could *descend* to *me*, or I could *rise* to *him*, which is utterly impossible.—Am I not unhappy enough in my Circumstances, without having an imprudent Inclination added to my other Misfortunes? Am I not destitute of Parents? And if I had any living, would they not blush to own me? And if Honour and Virtue allowed me to listen to Sir *George*, how could I bear to give Birth to Creatures only to make them as wretched as myself?——Here a Shower of Tears put a Stop to her Reflections, which she soon wiped away, and returned to her Needle with a Mind less disturbed.

Emily wrote again to Mrs. *Easy*, but only told her she was not with Mrs. *Freelove*, desired her Advice with Regard to *Hippocrene*, and begged to know when she intended to be in Town, not caring to to communicate all that had passed at *Fairly Manor* in a Letter, for fear it should miscarry, or be misinterpreted by her Friend, when she was at so great a Distance from her.

Emily lived in a very retired Manner above a Week, and stuck close to her Needle, not chusing to mix with the several Lodgers which were in the House with her. She was indeed rather reserved to Mrs. *Bond* herself, tho' very civil to her, because she did not like her so well as she did Mrs *Coleman*, but managed all her little Matters as well as she could in her own Room.

One Evening Mrs. *Bond*, having been told by her Maid, that *Emily* had made but a scanty Dinner, sent her up half a Chicken, an Apple-tart, and a Pint of White-wine, which she begg'd her to accept of. So large and so genteel a Present from a Woman in Mrs *Bond*'s middling Station of Life, surprized her prodigiously. She desired the Maid to carry it down again, and to tell her Mistress, that she had already supp'd, and would by no Means deprive her of so large a Share of her Repast.

Betty

Betty seemed very loth to carry it away, and said, her Mistress wou'd be very angry, and pressed *Emily* to accept of it, but she refused in so peremptory a Manner, that *Betty* went muttering down. In a short Time up came Mrs. *Bond* herself ——— La, Miss *Willis*, said she, why will you be so unkind as not to taste a bit of Supper? I wou'd have asked your Company below, but I thought that would not be so agreeable to you. Pray let me prevail on you to eat a bit, and drink a Glass of Wine, 'twill do you a great deal of Good, I dare say. Now I'll lay my Life I guess the Reason of your Refusal. You think I have been so extravagant as to buy all these Things; but you're mistaken now. They were presented to me by a Friend of mine, who, when she is in Town, is so good as to send me nice Things very often, and I am sure I know no Body more worthy to share them with me, than Miss *Willis*, so I beg you will sit down to them, and eat without Reserve. *Emily* returned her many Thanks, but desired to be excused, as she did not care for any Supper. Mrs. *Bond*, however, would take no Denial. She therefore just tasted the Chicken, but would

would not be prevailed upon to drink any Wine.

The next Day she received something, which at that Time she would have preferred to the most luxurious Banquet, a Letter from Mrs. *Easy*, which she unfolded with Transport, and which contained the following Lines.

" *To Miss* WILLIS.

" I WAS very glad, dear Miss *Willis*,
" to receive a Letter from you after
" so long a Silence, for which indeed
" I was a little angry with you: But
" I find you were not to blame. I have
" myself, in some Measure, occasioned
" the Interruption of our Correspon-
" dence, having been rambling about
" far from the Place I at first intended
" to stay at, and have but lately disco-
" vered that my Friend's Servant (whom
" she has just turned away) did not at-
" tend the Post-house so regularly as
" he should have done. I am both
" surprized and sorry that you have
" quitted *Fairly-Manor*, and am quite
" astonished at *Hippocrene*'s Voyage to
" *Ireland*, but can't tell how to offer
" you

" you Advice till I see you, which I
" hope will be in a few Days, at far-
" theſt, at my old Lodgings: Where
" no Body will be more ſincerely wel-
" comed than Miſs *Willis*,

" *By, her humble Servant,*

" A. EASY."

Emily was very glad to hear of her Friend's Intention of being in Town ſo ſoon, and ſat down to her Work with more Satisfaction than ſhe had felt, ſince her entering upon her new Way of Life. When ſhe had finiſhed the Shirts which Mrs *Bond* procured for her to make, that Gentlewoman preſſed her very much to carry them home herſelf, but ſhe wou'd by no Means liſten to her. I muſt beg the Favour of you, Madam, ſaid ſhe, to let your Servant carry them to the Gentleman, or to let them remain with you, till he ſends for them, as I don't think it prudent to go myſelf to a ſingle Man's Apartment I am not above my Buſineſs, Madam, continued ſhe, I wou'd wait upon any Lady with the greateſt Pleaſure, but I

had

had rather take lefs than the ufual Price for the Shirts I have made, than carry them home myfelf. Mrs. *Bond* made little or no Anfwer to this Speech, and *Emily* retired to her Chamber, where fhe continued to live very frugally, as fhe had but a fmall Quantity of Money, befides what fhe earn'd with her Fingers. Her good-natur'd Landlady frequently made her a Vifit, and attempted to make her feveral Prefents of Tea, Wine, and other Things, which fhe always faid had been given to her by her Friend. But *Emily* refufed them all, and began to fufpect, from fome Hints Mrs *Bond* threw out, at being fo often difconcerted, that there was a Plot carrying on againft her. Thefe Sufpicions put her upon her Guard, and made her think of looking out for another Lodging Juft at this Juncture, fhe received the following Card:

" Mrs. *Eafy* came to Town laft
" Night, and hopes Mifs *Willis* is well,
" and will be glad to fee her as foon as
" fhe can find an Opportunity."

Emily wanted no farther Invitation, but flew to her Friend, who received her in a very affectionate Manner, and again expressed her Concern, that their Correspondence had been so much interrupted. *Emily* then gave her a minute Detail of all that had happened to her since she left her, without suppressing even her Inclination for Sir *George*, and concluded with begging her Advice and Assistance.—I have no Reason, Miss *Willis*, said Mrs. *Easy*, to doubt the Truth of what you have been telling me, knowing, 'tis extremely difficult for such Girls as you to settle any where without those powerful Protectors of Youth and Innocence, good Parents, or good Husbands. But don't be discouraged, and look so dejected, I will do what I can for you. I wou'd advise you, in the first Place, to leave Mis *Bond*, for by your Account of her, I don't think you are safe in her House. As to Mrs. *Free'ove*, I don't know what to say I am afraid it will be an arduous Task, to endeavour to restore you to her Favour ——— Nor do I desire it, Madam, said *Emily*, for though I never have intentionally displeas'd her, I cou'd wish she was undeceiv'd with Regard to me, for I really love her; and tho' I am grieved to think she has so mean an Opinion

nion of me, I wou'd not chuse to live with her again, because I should then be exposed to the Sight of Sir *George*, whom I ought for ever to avoid.—You are in the right, Child, said Mrs *Easy*. I was afraid Something wrong wou'd happen there; but however, 'tis well Things are no worse than they are. You seem very sensible that Sir *George* must not be thought of by any Means, therefore I need not give you any Admonition on that Head; and as to *Hippocrene*, I will ask the Opinion of a Gentleman of my Acquaintance, as I am not much vers'd in Law-matters. Do you know to what Part of *Ireland* he is gone?— Mr. *M—tal* told me *Dublin*, Madam, said *Emily*, but he knows no more of him. —Then he might as well know nothing of him, said Mrs. *Easy.* But come, *Emily*, you must not cast yourself down, you're young, and must do the best you can for a Livelihood. What Way of Life now wou'd you chuse, if you had your little Fortune in your own Hands? —That Way, Madam, said *Emily*, in which you were so kind as to place me. I was compleatly happy with Mrs *Freelove* till Sir *George* came down.—Aye, but my Dear, said Mrs. *Easy*, there may be

be Sir *George*'s every where.—No, indeed, Madam, said *Emily*, I don't believe there is so amiable a Man in the World. I am sure, continued she, with a Sigh, I never met with such a one—Indeed, *Emily*, said Mrs. *Easy*, I wish you had never met with him, for he has made a most violent Impression on you, Child: But remember, you must endeavour to conquer it.—I will try to follow your Advice, Madam, said *Emily*, with the utmost Exactness, upon my Word I will.—Well then, said Mrs. *Easy*, you shall discharge your Lodging at Mrs. *Bond*'s, and occupy my Apartment till I return from *Kensington*, whither I am going for two or three Days with a Friend of mine. I will leave my Maid to wait upon you——Dear Madam, said *Emily*, how many Obligations am I under to you? You are my best, my only Friend.—Nay, Child, said Mrs. *Easy*, smiling, how can you talk of Obligations? 'Tis I that have brought you into all this *Embarrass*, but I am sure, I never intended it. And it may, perhaps, one Day or other turn out to your Advantage. We ought never to despair, 'tis both imprudent and irreligious. Providence often succours us
when

when we are prest by Dangers, and beset with Enemies, and when our Virtue, overwhelm'd with Grief, is just ready to sink, brings Relief by unforeseen Expedients. Keep up your Spirits therefore, my Dear, you deserve better Fortune: Continue to deserve it, by acting as prudently as you have done hitherto, and remember that there is no Happiness in this World without Virtue.———The Conversation then turned on the Revolutions at *Fairly-Manor*.

When *Emily* was going to take leave, about Dinner-time, Mrs. *Eafy* stopp'd her, and said, No, Miss *Willis*, you must dine with me To-day, and afterwards you shall go, if you please, to Mis *Bond*'s and fetch away your Things, then you may make my Lodgings your own, till my Return. I expect the Lady I am to go with, to call me at five o'Clock.— *Emily* obeyed her Friend with a great deal of Satisfaction.

When *Emily* paid off her Lodging, Mrs *Bond* seemed very loth to part with her, and began to sooth her with a great many flattering Speeches But her cool Behaviour soon put a Stop to them. She
desired

desired earnestly to know where *Emily* was going, but was again disappointed, for *Emily* only told her she was going to live with a Friend of hers. She then returned to Mrs. *Easy*, who set off, after an Hour's Chat, for *Kensington*. *Emily* could not help dropping a few Tears, when she saw the Coach drive from the Door, but wiped them soon, as she thought her Friend's Stay at the above mentioned Place would be short.

Emily continued a Week in her new Apartment, and was more cheerful than she had been since her Dismission from *Fanly-Manor*. Mrs *Easy* sent her a very long and friendly Letter, wherein she told her that she shou'd stay at *Kensington* longer than she intended, but that she shou'd certainly be in Town at the Beginning of the following Week. Her Letter concluded with this Paragraph. " I hope you will endeavour to amuse " yourself with Mrs *Coleman*, when you " want Company, for I can tell you she " has a great Regard for you."

Mrs. *Coleman* had indeed been prepossessed in Favour of *Emily* at first Sight, and had offered very likely to serve her as much as it lay in her Power; and *Emily* was the more inclin'd to believe what she said, as she seemed to be a very sedate, sensible Woman, and not originally designed to be the Mistress of a Lodging-house.

Mrs. *Coleman* was an old Acquaintance of Mrs *Easy*'s, and Wife of a Gentleman, whose Circumstances were once in a flourishing Way, but he had met with a Series of Misfortunes, and was now gone abroad to retrieve them. 'Twas Mrs *Easy* who put her upon taking a small House, and then rented the best Part of it, that it might be less expensive to her. She was therefore very obliging to Mrs *Easy* and her Friends, and was particularly pleased with *Emily*'s Company, whose Condition she pitied, tho' she knew nothing farther than that she was without Fortune and without Friends, and would be glad to get into some genteel Way of Life. Such was their Situation, when a Man left a Letter for *Emily*, two Days before Mrs *Easy*'s expected Return from *Kensington*. This Letter Mrs. *Coleman* herself gave to *Emily*, who cou'd not imagine from whom it came, as the Hand, Seal, and
Manner

Manner of Folding, were quite new to her. She retired, however, to her Chamber, in order to read it. As soon as she had opened it, she again recognized Sir *George*'s Hand. At first she resolved to seal it up, and send it back; but there was Something so bewitching in every Thing relating to Sir *George*, that she could not prevail on herself to let it go without a thorough Examination. But how great was her Surprize and Joy to read the following Lines!

" *To Miss* WILLIS.

" I Will not complain, Madam, of
" my Unhappiness, in being denied
" the Pleasure of seeing you, and even
" of affording you any Assistance in
" your Difficulties, since the Resolu-
" tion you have shewn to support your-
" self under them, and to refuse all im-
" proper Means of Relief, has made
" me still more acquainted with your
" boundless Merit, and has absolutely
" determin'd me to change the Senti-
" ments I have so long entertained
" against Matrimony. Permit me,
" therefore, my charming *Emily*, to
" beg your Acceptance of a Heart and
" Fortune

"Fortune, which shall always be en-
"tirely at your Disposal. And to con-
"vince you of the Sincerity of my In-
"tentions, I intreat you to consult your
"best Friends about fixing the Time
"and Place for the joining our Hands,
"which I desire may be in the most
"public Manner. My Estate is free
"from Incumbrances, and shall be
"settled on my *Emily* in the Manner
"she most approves of. My Family
"have no Right to dispute my Choice,
"nor can they make the least reasonable
"Objection to a Woman of your Figure
"and Education, who is form'd to
"adorn a much higher Station than
"it is in my Power to raise her to. My
"Heart is so full of the Happiness I
"hope soon to enjoy with my lovely
"Girl, that I cannot write correctly,
"nor tell her with my Pen all that I
"long to say to her. I hope you will
"now favour me with your Commands
"to wait upon you.—If this Request is
"too much to ask——if I must not be
"permitted to see you alone the first
"Time, let your kind Friend, with
"who you lodge, be present. This
"is certainly a reasonable Request,
"and therefore you will, I flatter my-
"self,

"self, comply with it ——I once fan-
"cied that I was not disagreeable to
"you,——but, perhaps, I was mis-
"taken —Cou'd you be witness to my
"Doubts and Fears, you wou'd pity
"me, I am sure you wou'd, and hasten,
"on the Wings of Good-nature, to
"relieve

" *Your most Faithful*

" *Humble Servant,*

" G. FREELOVE

" *P S.* My Servant will wait for an
" Answer."

Emily could scarce believe she was awake, and in her perfect Senses, so very unexpected were the Contents of this Letter. She read it over two or three Times, before she cou'd recover from the Flutter it had occasion'd, and think of answering it ——She wished most earnestly for her Friend Mrs *Eafy*, but as *her* Advice was not to be had at that Juncture, and as the Letter required an immediate Answer, she sat down to
her

her Desk, and after a little Demurring, wrote thus:

"*To Sir* GEORGE FREELOVE, *Bart.*

"SIR,

"YOU have done me so much Ho-
"nour, by the generous Proposal
"you have made me, and there appears
"so much Sincerity and Disinterested-
"ness in all that you have said on that
"Subject, that I will endeavour to
"follow so shining an Example, and
"deal with *you* as ingenuously as you
"have dealt with me. I think myself
"then, Sir, I once more assure you,
"highly honoured by the Offer you have
"made of your Heart and your For-
"tune: Yet, believe me, 'tis not the
"Title you are grac'd with, no the
"Estate you are possessed of, that wou'd
"induce me to receive the Hand you
"offer. 'Tis your Heart alone I prize;
"which I cou'd wish to be Mistress of,
"without those Appendages, which
"are, and must be, such formidable
"Bars to our Union. Be not displeased,
"Sir, with this frank Declaration—
"But be assured, I never will expose a
"Man, whom I have so much Reason
"to

"to esteem, to the Hatred and Con-
"tempt of his Family and his Friends.
"As to the Encomiums you so lavishly
"bestow on my Person and Education,
"they proceed from the too favourable
"Opinion *you* entertain of both ——
"But though you think so highly of
"me, your *Relations* never can. My
"unhappy, friendless Situation, and
"my Ignorance with Regard to the
"Authors of my Being, must inevi-
"tably render me despicable in *their*
"Eyes, and you will lessen yourself in
"their Esteem, by thinking on one so
"much beneath the Regard. And
"can I be deserving of your Love,
"when I am the Cause of your being
"the Object of their Ridicule and Con-
"tempt? No, Sir, Gratitude will not
"suffer me to act so base a Part. I am
"under infinite Obligations to you for
"your generous Intentions, but have
"nothing to do, but to wish that I was
"in a Situation which wou'd permit
"me to give my Hand to the only Man
"in the World who can give Happi-
"ness to,

"*Your obliged humble Servant,*
"E. W."

Poor *Emily* heav'd a Sigh and dropt a Tear at the Conclusion of her Letter, then sealed it, and gave it to Sir *George*'s Servant, who had waited for it above an Hour before she cou'd be satisfied with what she had written, or prevail on herself to let it go out of her Hands. As soon as it was gone past Recall, she unfolded Sir *George*'s Epistle again, which she perused with a melancholy Satisfaction. For while she admired the Contents of it, she cou'd not help lamenting her own unhappy Lot, which wou'd not suffer her to send an Answer more pleasing both to her Lover and herself. Yet why, said she, shou'd I deem myself wretched? I have arrived at the highest Pitch of Happiness that a Woman ought ever to aim at, for I am the free Choice of the most amiable of Men, and whom I have had the good Fortune to reclaim from the only Error he had fallen into. Let me, therefore, sit down contented with my Lot, and wish that my amiable Lover may enjoy all that Happiness with a more deserving Woman, which he generously intended to share with me. *Emily*, though she breathed out this Wish from the Bottom of her Heart, cou'd not think of resigning Sir *George*

George to another, without a Flood of Tears, and such discontented Exclamations as these, Oh how hard is my Fate!——What Pity is it that I must love and be unhappy!—With a Mind thus agitated by painful Reflections, she past a sleepless Night.—The next Morning Sir *George*'s Servant re-attended her with another Letter, which she opened with trembling Hands, and read as follows.

" *To Miss* WILLIS.

" I Was both surprized and grieved,
" my lovely *Emily*, to find so spirit-
" ed, and yet so cruel, an Answer to
" my last Letter: For though I was
" shock'd at your Refusal, I was struck
" with your Manner of expressing it.
" And must the most amiable Creature
" in the World raise my Esteem, and
" increase my Passion for her, at the
" same Time that she gives me no
" Hopes of a Return? No, Miss
" *Willis*—I cannot suffer you so en-
" chantingly to confess, that 'tis myself
" alone who can ever make you happy,
" and to discard me in the next Sen-
" tence by saying, that you imagine I
shall

"shall be lessened in the Eyes of my
"Family by so doing.—Do not har-
"bour such a Thought—nor believe
"that, while I am blest with my *Emily's*
"Love, the Behaviour of any other
"Person whatsoever, will give me a
"Moment's Uneasiness.—I again assure
"you, that my Estate is quite unen-
"cumbered: Nobody has the slightest
"Pretensions to oppose my Inclination
"in this, or any other Affair. My
"Aunt *Freelove* is indeed the only Rela-
"tion I have, who can claim the least
"Degree of Superiority over me. And
"even *she* was your Friend, and had a
"very sincere Regard for you, before
"that malicious Devil, Lady *Caroline*,
"stung with Envy and Jealousy, laid a
"Plot to ruin you in her Esteem, which
"succeeded too well. But I, by pre-
"ferring you to all your Sex, and by
"marrying you in the most public
"Manner, shall convince my Aunt, that
"I am satisfied you have been most
"scandalously abused. This step of
"mine will restore you to her Favour
"and Affection, and make a considera-
"ble Addition to our mutual Felicity.
"—Be not afraid then, my dearest
"*Emily*, lest any of my Family should
"reasonably

"reasonably object to our Union.—And
"if they act *unreasonably*, they ought
"not to be regarded. Nor think that
"an obscure Birth, (supposing that to
"be your Case, which I own I can't
"believe) can make you more or
"less deserving in the Opinion of un-
"derstanding People. When Persons
"derive mean Notions and Manners
"from a mean Extraction, and are
"thereby influenced to act meanly,
"such an Alliance with them is not to
"be wished for. But those who have had
"a liberal Education, who are possessed
"of good Talents, and who know how
"to conduct themselves with Propriety,
"may be raised to the most exalted
"Stations with Honour, and we often
"see such Persons acquit themselves to
"the utter Shame of those who are
"much more illustriously born.—Let
"these Reflections then, my dearest
"*Emily*, convince you that you ought
"not to listen to these idle Surmises,
"but to reject them immediately, and
"consent to be mine for ever. You
"say, you wish to make me happy.—
"Do it then, my Angel, for 'tis only
"in *your* Power.—Give me Leave to
"see you this Evening, and let me have

the

" the Satisfaction to hear that all your
" Scruples are at an End—And believe
" me to be, in the mean Time,

" *Your most sincere Admirer,*

" *And Faithful humble Servant,*

" G. FREELOVE."

Emily was shock'd at the Receipt of Sir *George*'s *first* Letter, but still more so at the Receipt of *this*, for it almost deprived her of the Powers of Reflection. —She sat near an Hour before she cou'd think of answering it; but when her Maid told her the Servant who brought it grew impatient, she snatch'd up her Pen, and wrote the following Answer.

" *To Sir* GEORGE FREELOVE, *Bart.*

" S I R,

" IF you have the least Regard for
" me, I intreat you to put an im-
" mediate Stop to our Correspondence
" I sent you my Thoughts very freely in
" my last Letter, hoping they would be
" satisfactory, but since they are not,
" and

" and since I am likely to be drawn into
" a Debate with you upon very une-
" qual Terms, give me Leave only to
" add one substantial Reason to those I
" have already mentioned, for declining
" the Honour you are so solicitous to
" confer on me —— Mrs *Freelove* be-
" lieves that I am capable of having a
" Design upon your Title and Fortune.
" —Were I to accept of your Offer, her
" Suspicions would be confirmed.——
" And not only her's, but the Suspici-
" ons of all your Friends and Acquain-
" tance. Neither Honour nor Prudence
" therefore, Sir, will permit me to en-
" courage your Addresses; nor to re-
" ceive any more Letters from you,
" which must be returned unopened for
" the future. I shall always, however,
" sincerely wish you the greatest Hap-
" piness, and esteem myself

" *Your most obliged*

" *Humble Servant*

" E. W."

End of the FIRST VOLUME.

Just Published,

(In Three Volumes, Price 9s. Bound,)

THE

PERPLEXED LOVERS;

OR, THE

HISTORY

OF

S. EDWARD BALCHEN, Bart.

Printed for F. and J. NOBLE.